BRIAN K. MILFORD
EDITOR

HOLY CONTRADICTIONS

WHAT'S NEXT FOR THE PEOPLE CALLED UNITED METHODISTS

ABINGDON PRESS
NASHVILLE

HOLY CONTRADICTIONS:
WHAT'S NEXT FOR THE PEOPLE CALLED UNITED METHODISTS

This book is printed on elemental chlorine-free paper.

ISBN 9781501859717

Scott Kisker's essay, "Unity with Division: John Wesley on the Church," originally appeared under the title "Applying What Wesley Taught about Schism" in *Circuit Rider*, vol. 41, no. 4, August/September/October 2017.

Magrey deVega's essay, "The Ethics of Love," originally appeared in *Hyde Park UMC News,* May 11, 2017, "All News, Midweek Message, Top News" — http://hydeparkumc.org/midweek-message-broad-center-church/# and is used by permission.

18 19 20 21 22 23 24 25 26 27 — 10 9 8 7 6 5 4 3 2 1

MANUFACTURED IN THE UNITED STATES OF AMERICA

Contents

Introduction

JAZZ IS A UNIQUE MUSICAL genre. It has multiple origins and includes several sub-genres. Improvisation with its creativity and unpredictability is one of its key elements. Performers of classical music are mostly evaluated by their ability to master a musical score and its prescribed arrangements, while many jazz musicians don't follow a score. Instead, they pay close attention to and interact with one another in real time.

Jazz depends on creativity, interplay, and collaboration as the members of a group contribute from their diversity to achieve coherence and ultimate resolution. The ability of highly skilled jazz musicians to appreciate the gifts of their colleagues, respond appropriately, and move the performance forward is a metaphor for how the Holy Spirit blends myriad elements to bear fruit as order, unity, and faithfulness through human encounters.

Kamasi Washington is a saxophonist and composer whose compositions, performances, and spiritual approach all display how forces that seem to be working in opposition can come together in an integrated experience of complex beauty. Regarding his album *Harmony of Difference*, Washington states, "My hope is that witnessing the beautiful harmony created by merging different musical melodies will help realize the beauty in our own differences."

The essays in this book describe different views at a particular moment in time in the life of The United Methodist Church. The General Conference of 2016 asked the Council of Bishops to lead the church in finding a way forward on matters of human sexuality, and the special called General Conference (a rare occurrence) in 2019 will receive and act on the Council of Bishops' report, based on the work of the Commission on a Way Forward.

We recognize that the tensions we currently face in The UMC are in part denominational expressions of underlying cultural and worldwide stresses in the social order and in how the church plays a role in defining and advancing civic virtue and social justice. Thus the presenting issues are larger than questions about human sexuality and sexual ethics, but for United Methodists they will not be faithfully addressed without acknowledging the diversity of convictions that exist around these specific matters. By seeking to discern and grapple with how these topics intersect with our core mission, United Methodists provide a powerful example and healing witness to a divided world.

We invited essayists to answer this question: *How might United Methodists bear witness to graceful and mutually respectful ways of living in the Wesleyan tradition amid enduring disagreements about same-gender relationships and related church practices?* The writers considered the question in light of their particular location (pastor, leader, disciple, young person); identified what is most at stake, most at risk, and most needed at this time in the life of The UMC; and reflected on how their understanding of Holy Scripture and Our Theological Task *(The Book of Discipline)* should guide how we live together.

You will sense in these essays the writers' deep and abiding love for The UMC. You will note their unwavering commitment to the task of making disciples of Jesus Christ for the transformation of the world. So why do we call this collection *Holy Contradictions*? Because you will also find perspectives that both challenge and reinforce your ways of thinking. You will encounter advocates with a passion for evangelism and for justice; note examples of a shared appreciation for biblical authority that lead to quite different conclusions about biblical interpretation; observe that some emphasize unconditional grace, while others focus on the process of sanctification; detect that some pay more attention to personal holiness and others to social action; and find that several express abiding respect for the existing contents of *The Book of Discipline*, the Doctrinal Standards, and Our Theological Task, while others cry out for what they view as necessary and overdue changes.

As you read these essays, ask yourself the same question the writers have wrestled with: *How might United Methodists bear witness to graceful and mutually respectful ways of living in the Wesleyan tradition amid enduring disagreements about same-gender relationships and related church practices?*

How will "all this jazz" come together to represent the beauty of diversity and multiple contributions in the life of The United Methodist Church? How will you help shape the composition and participate in its performance? Where will this musical experience find richly resonant resolution in 2019 and beyond?

God will ultimately bring us home. How will that be expressed as the music unfolds?

—Brian K. Milford
Publisher
Abingdon Press

1

All Holy . . . All Beloved

M. Garlinda Burton

M. Garlinda Burton is a United Methodist deaconess based in Nashville. She is program director for the Nashville Freedom School Partnership and a resource development director for the denomination's General Commission on Religion and Race.

HAVING A COMMUNITY OF PEOPLE who share faith and who share a common sense of justice can be like an island of respite and calm in turbulent seas. And those of us who engage in justice work usually find ourselves in turbulent seas. God has created communities to help us refocus and refuel so we can go back out into the world and proclaim the Christ who has saved and claimed as precious every human being on this earth.

In the context of refocusing and refueling that we seem to need in this time in the life of our church, I am encouraged, challenged, and inspired by Psalm 146:

Happy are those whose help is the God of Israel,
whose hope is in [the Sovereign God],
who made heaven and earth,
the sea and all that is in them!
[God], you keep faith forever:
you secure justice for the oppressed;
you give food to the hungry;
you set the captives free;

you give sight to the blind;
you raise up those who were bowed down;
you love those who do justice;
you protect strangers;
you sustain orphans and the bereaved—.
but you thwart the way of the corrupt.
God will reign forever—your God, Zion!—
through all generations. Alleluia!
(Psalm 146:5-10, The Inclusive Bible*)*

This psalm is encouraging, because it reminds us that God has already done a lot of our work. This psalm tells us the end of the struggle and the end of the story: love wins!

And so, by comparison, the tasks left to us seem relatively simple. We merely have to do God's justice, echo God's mercy, and walk humbly with the One who has already set the agenda, drawn up the blueprints, redeemed us, and who has even written the end of the story. And my message is this: We must stay the course and rock and roll The United Methodist Church until full justice for LGBTQ persons is realized.

We must stay focused on the ministry of Christian social justice for marginalized people until marginalized people are no longer marginalized. And as we open doors for lesbian, gay, bisexual, transgender, intersex, queer, and questioning brothers and sisters, we must remember and remind others to ensure that no one shuts those doors and cuts off conversations just because "our people" have made it through.

We keep telling ourselves that all people are of sacred worth, but—! And this is not the first time in our history that there were people stuck behind the *but*. Sacred, but the wrong social class. Sacred, but the wrong color. Sacred, but too young. Sacred, but not enough money. There is no "but" in God's agenda. In creating us in the divine image, God declared from the beginning of time that *all* people are of sacred worth—period. No *ifs, ands,* or *buts*. So ordination, licensing, and the right to marry and raise children are not limited by God to one gender identity or one sexual orientation. That's what is written on God's agenda. Our baptism has marked us for life as belonging to God. As Bill McElvaney wrote in *Becoming a Justice-Seeking Congregation,* "Baptism . . . is our identification card . . . our spiritual, theological MasterCard. We do well not to leave home without it."[1]

So those of us who are engaged in the work of freeing the church from homophobia, heterosexism and gender-identity myopia only have to live out and act out our baptism. We are *all* created in God's image, we are *all* sacred, and while—yes, annual conferences have the right to set standards for ministry—"standards" and "unjust biases" are not the same thing. *All* means *all.*

We cannot help God transform a world we don't recognize or respect or revere. Why would a person our church doesn't acknowledge as God's own marvelous creation want to join our church?

No matter what we say, or put in a resolution, or repeat in our weekly rituals, justice is not just a badge that can be put on and taken off. Mere statements and attitudes and wearing a rainbow stole do not point to authenticity and sincerity of the church and our message. No matter how many times some church folks claim that they "love the sinner; hate the sin," or that a holy love between same-sex couples is "incompatible with Christian teaching," or say, "You have sacred worth, *but,*" those on the margins hear: "God's love and justice and righteousness don't roll down for you—you have to settle for the trickle-down leftovers." And that is not the God of David's song.

To quote McElvaney again, "If our interpretation of God's voice does not point to a God of love and justice, a God of truth and peace, and to our being called to respond accordingly,"[2] then the church needs to stop trying to make statements about it, be quiet and listen more earnestly and push our biased egos out of the way until we can again hear the true voice of the God of Gomer and Hosea, of Ruth and Boaz, and of Jonathan and David. We need to listen anew to the God who not only included in the holy books stories of nuclear, heterosexual, no sex-until-marriage-to-a-virgin love, but love and sexual love in more than one incarnation.

As we walk hand-in-hand with God, we also must see our work as part of the larger work of God's coming to earth and understand that "marginalization" and "injustice" refer to the LGBTQ community and to many who are in other-than-the-LGBTQ community. And if we are truly called to ministry on the margins, then we must also champion and be drum majors for righteousness throughout the human community.

Writer Evelyn Underhill says that if we are truly engaged with God in transforming the world, then our spirituality must be *"larger, fuller, richer, more generous in its interests than the interests of the natural life alone can ever be; must invade and transform all homely activities and practical things. For it means an offering of life to the [God] of life, to Whom it all belongs; a willingness—an eager willingness—to take our small place in the vast operations of [God's] Spirit instead of trying to run a poky little business on our own."*[3] These words serve as a reminder that if we dare to narrow God's definition of and God's agenda for justice, we do so at a great risk of missing the message and missing the opportunity to change more than just one area of injustice.

Consider how badly the church historically has narrowed and mangled the lessons from the Bible. The story of Sodom and Gomorrah is used selectively and narrowly to beat up on gay folks, but what gets missed is that women were so devalued by our biblical ancestors that their father, Lot, was willing to send his own daughters out to be raped and brutalized by ruffians to protect strangers he didn't even know. Admirable? Not when you're the daughters.

Ruth, the Moabitess, was from an ethnic minority; and had not Boaz and Naomi orchestrated her marriage into their family, Ruth would have been subject to racial and religious persecution and sexual violence at the hands of God's so-called chosen.

In both of these cases, people who called themselves God's own—who themselves who had been saved by God from oppression, hunger, and marginalization—then participated in the marginalization of others. That's what happens when God's agenda of justice is reduced to "just us."

Black Christian preachers are among some of the most homophobic and sexist folk I have ever met. I am a product of the black church from whence the Civil Rights movement was born, from whence came Martin Luther King, Jr., and Fannie Lou Hamer and Gil Caldwell and Pamela Lightsey. But as we worked and continue to struggle for rights for black folks, our leaders in many instances have failed to hold up the larger vision of freedom and equality for women, for LBGTQ folks, for young people. And some of us are as cold and indifferent as any white Christians to the cries of poor black and brown sisters and brothers. That is what happens when we fail to embrace God's larger agenda of proclaiming release to *all* captives, and jubilee for *all* who are cast out, and opening doors for *all* who are pushed aside.

By the same token, too often when I'm involved in Reconciling Ministries work, if I didn't know better I would think that there are *no* black, brown, golden, or red or interracial or poor or lesbian, gay, bisexual, transgender, or intersexed folks in this community. And that's a concern I hear repeated among those of us who declare ourselves allies for LGBTQ persons and allies for women, for children, for people of color, for the poor.

How wide is God's love? How wide is our love?

Are we really just facing a choice between being either racist or homophobic? It is as if we serve a one-note God for whom the words *diversity* and *inclusiveness* can only mean "*my* folks." But that doesn't sound like the Almighty God to whom David sang.

I believe in full rights for LGBTQ folks in The United Methodist Church and in larger society. As a Christian who has studied Scripture and has engaged in prayer and Holy Conversation, I believe that same-sex love, like heterosexual love, is compatible with the teachings of Jesus Christ and even the Old Testament. I think the current church teaching is just plain wrong, and that it is time to declare that.

At the same time, I believe that justice for LGBTQ folks is also an important step in the continuing journey of tearing down walls of hatred, bigotry, fear, and wrong-headed biblical and theological interpretation in order to free *all* people who are oppressed, marginalized, and treated as "less than." This work does not end as soon as middle-class, white LGBTQ persons are included and respected as sacred. This work must continue until girls in Nigeria do not risk their lives just to get an education. This work must continue until a living wage is secured as a right not a perk. This work must continue until women around the world earn dollar for dollar what a man earns, from the factory floor to the local church. This work must continue until black and Latino boys in this country are not bred like cattle to feed a cradle-to-grave prison-as-profit system.

This work must continue until we—God's holy church—no longer have to name one group as having sacred worth, but show the world by our living and our loving that God made each one of us sacred and holy and beloved beyond price.

NOTES

1. William K. McElvaney, *Becoming a Justice-Seeking Congregation: Responding to God's Justice Initiative,* (Bloomington IN: iUniverse, 2009), 32.
2. Ibid., 26–27.
3. Evelyn Underhill, *Advent with Evelyn Underhill,* edited by Christopher L. Webber (Harrisburg PA: Morehouse Publishing, 2006), 21.

2

Mutually Respectful Ways of Living

Bryan D. Collier

Bryan D. Collier is founding and lead pastor at The Orchard, Tupelo, Mississippi.

I AM NO LONGER A United Methodist pastor, and the church I pastor is no longer a United Methodist church. For this reason, I initially balked at the invitation to contribute to this volume. However, when the publisher reached out to me a second time—assuring me that they had taken this fact into consideration—and invited me to reconsider joining the conversation, I accepted. Primarily, my motivation in participating was the opportunity to have a civil conversation about the topic assigned in each of these essays: *How might United Methodists bear witness to graceful and mutually respectful ways of living in the Wesleyan tradition amid enduring disagreements about same-gender relationships and related church practices?* Assuming that all of the essayists have given up hope of ever persuading those they disagree with to see it their way on this matter, it is intriguing to consider graceful and respectful ways forward given our disagreements. During my twenty-five years in United Methodist ministry, this conversation and the pursuit of this idea were absent far more than present in our shared lives together, and the chance to speak and listen was too rich too pass up.

One might think that my leaving the denomination was an occasion of hostility, vitriol, and hard feelings. Nothing could be further from the truth. My exit and the exit of our congregation came after years of groaning and much grief, and our prayers and love for our United Methodist brothers and sisters are unwavering. The fact is we just could not live with the church anymore. That is a stark statement, I know, but it is honest; and the consequence of coming to that reality was freeing and painful at the same time. The decision came after three months of fasting and praying by our pastors and leaders and after an additional four months of discernment conversations with our annual conference. It was not a reflection of my annual conference's leadership, but came out of the conviction that the upcoming argument around the election of Karen Oliveto as bishop in the Western Jurisdiction and The United Methodist Church's position on human sexuality was going to reach a fever pitch that would be harmful to our witness, dishonoring to God, and disrespectful of our UM brothers and sisters. We had no desire as a church to participate in that kind of process.

One phrase in the assigned topic captured me and is the title I chose for my essay: ". . . mutually respectful ways of living. . . ." This phrase embodies our congregation's approach to living in the four communities where we are located. And the reason that it embodies our approach is that it is woven into our very DNA. It is not something we do; it is who we are. This way of living in ministry, however, causes extreme conflict in several ways within United Methodism, and this poses a problem in answering the question of how we can live in a mutually respectful way.

The first point of conflict surrounds the degree of importance attached to same-gender relationships and related church practices. For many churches and pastors this is a gospel *issue,* but for many others this *is* the gospel itself. The gospel by its claims drives us to the issue of all the dimensions of human sexuality, but this issue is not the gospel itself or even the central kernel of it. For our church this is an important matter, but it is not the *ultimate* matter that many on both sides of the issue have made it. The mission of the church, given in the Scriptures, is to preach the gospel and make disciples; but that has gotten lost in our making sexuality matters the litmus test of whether someone actually believes and practices our version of the gospel. This is not to say that because this is not the ultimate matter that it is not an important matter. The problem in our church is that it has become the dominating matter to the point of distraction. My position and The Orchard's position is that Scripture has settled this and that *The Book of Discipline* in its current form agrees that Scripture has settled this, and for that reason we should set aside the distraction and get on with the work of ministry. But we can't because both sides feel the stakes are too high. This says nothing of the root issue in our disagreement about human sexuality—the role and authority of Scripture. So not only can we not agree on the issue; we cannot agree on what will be the authority and final word on the issue.

The second point of conflict in this matter is that we do not live in a mutually respectful way in this conversation. Over the twenty-five years I was engaged in United Methodist ministry, our living and conversation around this matter has not become more civil; it has become more hostile, and that hostility continues to increase. Certainly there is a moderate middle, and both extremes are angered by their seeming inability to take a position. But that middle is bleeding to the edges because the pressure to take a position on one end or the other of the conversation is enormous. Because each side feels the need to build its "army," the recruitment and training is intense; and the sides only grow further apart and further away from any hope of civil conversation about the way forward. I liken the whole tenor of the United Methodist family to a couple in conflict whose relationship continues to become more hostile. Though separation is regrettable, less than God intended and worthy of grieving, it is still better than the harm they are doing to each other. I will admit that this metaphor breaks down a bit because divorce is sin, and I do not believe that churches that divorce themselves from the denominational are sinful. However, if we can agree that most pastors would not advise a couple embroiled in hostility to continue living together, maybe we can agree that the partners in this hostile relationship would be better off apart.

However, taking our own advice about separation has its own problems. Aside from acknowledging this is not God's ideal and acknowledging our regret and grief, there is currently no way to peaceably withdraw or separate from one another. This may be more telling than we want to admit. When The Orchard began the conversation about peacefully withdrawing from The United Methodist Church, I approached Bishop James Swanson of the Mississippi Area and asked him about "peacefully withdrawing." He acknowledged that there was no process in *The Book of Discipline* for doing so—that the only way was the closing of the local church. While this seems simple enough, a quick read-through reveals that the process is centered around negotiations and legal matters in a way that is inherently tense and hostile. So even if we could agree that some distance and separation around this matter was desired, under the current covenant we cannot get there. To the credit of the Mississippi Annual Conference officials and the leadership of The Orchard, the process of ending our relationship remained honorable, respectful, and kind toward one another. This is not to say that there was no tension or difficult moments; but both parties deeply wanted to model a peaceful, respectful process because we care about one another and about our witness as we worked through our disagreement. Regrettably, there is no process that allows for this. It must be made up as we go if the parties can agree that they want to act in ways that are mutually respectful toward one another.

Finally, though I am sure there are many other points that cause conflict, we disagree so sharply theologically on this matter that acquiescence by either side seems like giving up their faith. John's Gospel announces that Jesus was full of grace and truth (John 1:14). This same characteristic is true of the church that is engaged in the ministry of Jesus. However, as broken people of faith we tend to err on one extreme or the other. Some people tend to be full of grace at the expense of truth; this leads to permissiveness. Others tend to be full of truth at the expense of grace; this leads to legalism. Neither side sees its weakness or is willing to engage the other in growing in understanding and practice in this area of weakness. Grace people believe that the way to extend grace is to change the truth; truth people often wait to extend grace as reward for obedience to truth. Both approaches are theological malpractice for people who are called to be *full* of grace and *full* of truth. In *My Utmost for His Highest,* Oswald Chambers wrote, "The characteristic of the holiness which is the outcome of the indwelling of God is a blazing truthfulness with regard to God's word and an amazing tenderness in personal dealing."[1] Chambers' remarks echo Jesus' nature and practice of being full of grace and truth. As people of Jesus, we are called to stand with a blazing passion for God's word (truth) and an amazing compassion for all people (grace). I believe we could wrestle with what grace looks like if we agree on what truth looks like, but we don't agree on either.

These points of contention and the inability of the denomination to have civil conversations around them are ultimately what led The Orchard to decide that the only way to live in mutually respectful ways was to peacefully withdraw. I have said many times that neither I nor The Orchard is advocating that this should be everyone's response. We have not tried in any way to coach or coax other churches to follow our lead. This was the right decision for our church. We cannot say that it would be the right decision for other churches. But for the sake of this essay, I want to suggest that this may be the only way for United Methodists to live together in mutually respectful ways as we go forward. The points of conflict I outline above are growing, not subsiding. The decision to peacefully withdraw did not come quickly or easily for us. My personal heritage is in Methodism for over a century. The Orchard's roots and grounding have been there since its beginning. But the growing conflict had become so distracting that ministry was being hindered, so we began examining our options. I believe for the sake of our witness and the practice of ministry, United Methodism should do the same.

Certainly our first option was to stay and fight. However, though this matter is of significant importance to us, the energy, money, and effort to engage in a theological fight were deterrents to choosing this option. We just want to do ministry in Jesus' name. We wanted to do ministry as a United Methodist Church, but to do so was to choose to fight, pick a side, and engage the other viciously to get our way. Another option was passivity. We could have kept our heads down and let someone else fight while we did ministry. We could have withheld our apportionments, another passive move; refused to serve on boards and agencies; and just taken care of ourselves and our communities. However, to be part of a family means to engage and participate; therefore, this option did not seem faithful to us. So that left us with withdrawal. We decided to not stay in a family with growing hostility among its family members. We decided not to stay in a family where we pretend to be a part by retaining the name, but only passively or sparingly engaging. We decided to withdraw, and I believe this is what congregations and pastors on either side of the debate who cannot live mutually respectful lives together must do.

Of course, with considering this option, we also considered the consequences. Chief among these consequences was loss of relationship. Like any family member who no longer wants to be part of the family, we anticipated being treated as though we were dead. We also anticipated anger, false accusations, misunderstanding, and hostile attacks. We received all of those. We also received words of sorrow, grief, and loss, and we hurt with those who hurt for the loss of relationship. United Methodism truly is a family. We also anticipated some positive outcomes—primarily, the absence of debate and distraction. These have been felt as well. In the months since we left, I can honestly say that there is a freedom in ministry that I have never experienced before. We have not debated or thought about the denominational firestorm that most of our friends are experiencing except to pray for them and The United Methodist Church. We have been focused on the ministry of Jesus locally, regionally, and globally around all the matters of faith—including those of human sexuality.

Ultimately, our decision to withdraw was in order to maintain our witness to an unbelieving world in the face of what we believed would be mutually dishonoring and disrespecting ways. We see no way for the bishops' Commission on a Way Forward to come to a decision that will lead to a peaceable way forward. With that conviction, it is my belief that the only way to live together in mutually respectful ways is to live separately. It is not unusual for people to have good relationships with people they disagree sharply with; however, reasonable relational distance is necessary for the health of that relationship. For United Methodists, living in the same house is not reasonable relational distance. Peaceful separation before our relationship becomes so hostile that peace is not an option seems to be the surest road.

Certainly there are those who will disagree with me. Unity at any cost. Family at any cost. However, family cannot exist without trust—and there is no trust. The theological process is an essential part of any denominational family; but in order for family to continue to be family and not enemy, there have to be mutually respectful ways of not only living together but also of talking together about vital matters—and currently there is no way of doing that. I believe that every church and pastor would like to have freedom of conversation without debate and loss of relationship. I am just not sure that is possible within the UM family anymore. If the Commission cannot come up with a solution where we can stop debating this issue and still live in relationship, then we are only left with two options: remain in a relationship where hatred, vitriol, and demonizing the other continue or peacefully withdraw. The mission is too important; relationship is too important. The Orchard made its choice believing that the only way to live together in mutually respectful ways is to create some relational distance by peacefully withdrawing. This may be the only way forward for the United Methodist family to live together in mutually respectful ways.

NOTES

1. Oswald Chambers, *Still Higher for His Highest* (Grand Rapids, MI: Zondervan, Revised, 1989), 235–236.

3

Thoughts on a Way Forward

Jim and Jennifer Cowart

Jim and Jennifer Cowart are lead and founding pastor and executive pastor, respectively, of Harvest Church in Warner Robins, Georgia.

Unity . . . but Not at Any Price

UNITY SEEMS TO BE A high priority for The United Methodist Church. And rightly so. We certainly need unity in the local church and the denomination. Our bishops speak of it often; and it's a resounding theme for the very existence of the Commission on a Way Forward. But when unity becomes the prime directive, there is a danger of something being lost. If all our attention and drive are toward unity alone, then collateral damage and unforeseen implications can occur. To many of us in the local church, the message coming from denominational leaders sounds like, "Hold the UM structure together . . . at all costs!"

But if we lose faithfulness, that's too high a price to pay! Without faithfulness, unity doesn't happen and can't really exist—in a friendship, a marriage, a church, a denomination, or with God. After all, we are people of the covenant. Covenants are meant to be kept by all parties involved. In the Old and New Testaments we see God use the word *if* in regard to covenant relationships. "Today I am giving you the choice between a blessing and a curse! You will be *blessed if* you obey the commands of the LORD your God that I am giving you today. But you will be *cursed if* you reject the commands of the LORD." (Deuteronomy 11:26-28 NLT, emphasis added).

Throughout the Scriptures we see this "promise with a premise" repeated. Our covenant relationship with God is based on this. There is a premise for us to meet in order for the promise to be fulfilled. God has a part, and we have a part. We can't have real unity with God if we continue to disobey his commands and refuse to return to him in obedience. And we cannot have real unity in The United Methodist Church if we can't determine what faithfulness means or if we refuse to do it. When unity becomes our foremost ambition, other values that are essential—such as faithfulness—can be overlooked. The result is that the form of unity achieved is a pale imitation of the real thing.

Redefining Key Words

We've seen several key words tossed around in the last few years and used somewhat out of context. *Tolerance* is one of these words. The definition of the word means that we treat others with dignity and respect, even when we disagree. It is an admirable attitude to have toward others. But in recent years, some have tried to change *tolerance* to mean all ideas are of equal value. And that's just not true. When someone holds to a value that we disagree with, we can and should still treat that person with respect. However, we cross the line when, in disagreement, we expect not only respect, but also approval from those who disagree with us. That's not *tolerance* anymore, but something far less noble and far more selfish.

Schism is another one of these words. *Schism* means to separate or divide with toxic or manipulative attitude or actions. Personally, we hope and pray for The UMC to stay together; to live together in unity with integrity. But as we search for a way forward, this word *schism* is sometimes tossed like a hand grenade from one side to the other, as if talking about separating in good faith is a *schism*. It is not. Take Abram and Lot, for example. "So Abram said to Lot, 'Let's not have any quarreling between you and me. . . . Is not the whole land before you? Let's part company. If you go to the left, I'll go to the right . . . " (Genesis 13:8-9 NIV). Then in Acts 15, we see the separation of Paul and Barnabas because they cannot come to a compromise about taking John

Mark on a missionary journey. "Their disagreement was so sharp that they separated" (Acts 15:39*a* NLT).

Neither of these separations was schism. They talked, discussed, debated, and then determined that separation seemed the best option. Again, we hope we find a way to stay together. But if we can't, we must be able to talk with one another about separation without accusing each other of intentionally causing schism.

Disagree without Becoming Disagreeable

A world that needs Jesus is watching the United Methodist family argue. We should be concerned and embarrassed by what they are seeing on social media and network news. Even in disagreement, we should be treating one another with dignity and respect. We need to learn how to disagree without becoming disagreeable. Here's a little quadrant to help us as we seek to disagree in a faithful way.

Noble Correct	Noble Incorrect
Abrasive Correct	Abrasive Incorrect

Someone is right and someone is wrong in this theological debate regarding same-gender issues. Both sides can't be right, and yet both sides of the debate feel passionately. So consider these definitions; not to solve the debate but to guide us in how we debate one another.

Noble Correct: correct theologically while treating others with dignity and respect

Noble Incorrect: incorrect theologically while treating others with dignity and respect

Abrasive Correct: correct theologically but being a jerk about it

Abrasive Incorrect: incorrect theologically and being a jerk about it

We study Scripture, pray, and make the best decision we can to be correct. But we might miss it. What we can definitively decide, however, is to *live above the line*. We can choose to be noble with our words, actions, and attitudes. If we are wrong, then let us be sincerely wrong. But let us not wound with our words or actions and hurt brothers and sisters in Christ, or someone who needs Christ.

Why So Offended?

Personally, we believe that the Bible teaches that the practice of homosexuality is a sin. To say that in today's politically charged culture can bring cries of outrage and ridicule. Some have even suggested that the use of the word *sin* should fall into the category of a hate crime. Why is that?

If you disagree with our position, we don't hate or fear you. We are not interested in trying to force you to change your opinion. But that goes both ways.

Live by the Rules, Change the Rules, or Go in Peace

Here's an honest frustration with our progressive clergy friends regarding the same-gender issue. You knew where this plane was going when you got on it. The United Methodist stance on homosexuality has been consistent for decades. When you were ordained, you said you agreed with The UMC rules of order and vowed to uphold them. Much of the debate and disobedience from those who would change the *Book of Discipline* regarding homosexuality feels like a hijacking. Think about it. If you get on a flight scheduled from Atlanta to L.A. and in mid-flight try to alter the route to Dallas, it's called hijacking. If you want to go to Dallas, that's fine. But the rest of us are trying to get to L.A. There are flights to Dallas. Get on one of those.

For decades The UMC has discussed, debated, and voted on the issue of homosexuality. There has been consistency in our direction. The policy stated in the *Book of Discipline* reflects an attitude of genuine respect and concern for persons with same-gender attraction. Here are the words again:

> We affirm that all persons are individuals of sacred worth, created in the image of God. All persons need the ministry of the Church in their struggles for human fulfillment, as well as the spiritual and emotional care of a fellowship that enables reconciling relationships with God, with others, and with self. The United Methodist Church does not condone the practice of homosexuality and considers this practice incompatible with Christian teaching. We affirm that God's grace is available to all. We will seek to live together in Christian community, welcoming, forgiving, and loving one another, as Christ has loved and accepted us. We implore families and churches not to reject or condemn lesbian and gay members and friends. We commit ourselves to be in ministry for and with all persons. (*The Book of Discipline of The United Methodist Church,* 2016, ¶161.G)

The current statement is both clear and loving. It draws a distinction between *acceptance* and *approval.* In John 8, we see Jesus' encounter with a woman caught in adultery. We are told that the scribes and Pharisees use this woman as a test in hopes of catching Jesus in a moral conundrum between grace and the law. But Jesus will not be trapped. He first speaks to the crowd asking for the woman's execution, "He who is without sin among you, let him throw a stone at her first." Thinking about this, the crowd soon disperses, leaving the woman alone. He then says to her, "Neither do I condemn you; go and sin no more" (John 8:7, 11 NKJV). These two responses are filled with both grace and truth.

To the crowd: Don't throw stones.

To the woman: I don't condemn you either. Go and change your lifestyle.

This blend of grace and truth is found in our current wording of the *Book of Discipline* regarding the practice of homosexuality. We must love people. We must not throw stones literally or metaphorically with condemnation. But we must also speak the truth in love. Again, for the conservative believer, that truth is found in Scripture. Sex is reserved for a relationship between one man and one woman in marriage.

There is a difference between *acceptance* and *approval*. We can accept people who are far from God. Our churches should be places where we reach out to the messy, the hurting, and the lost. Acceptance says, "You are welcome here just the way you are. You don't have to clean yourself up or get your life together to come in to this place." But . . . if we really love people, we do not condone or overlook sin or choices that are harmful. We can accept people without approving of lifestyle choices. The job of the church is to help people repent and begin a relationship with God through Jesus.

Jesus accepted the woman caught in adultery. He didn't make her get baptized or put on nice clothes before he talked to her. He loved and accepted her in her current condition. But he didn't say, "That's okay. Culture is more open to your lifestyle now. You can keep on having affairs and God will love and forgive you." No. He said, "Go and sin no more." Stop doing that.

Real love does not approve every behavior. Real love points out sinful habits and holds accountable. We must love with great compassion, *and* we must speak the truth in love.

To those who would change the stance of The UMC regarding homosexuality we would ask, "And then what? Is the goal to remove from society any mention or concept of the word *sin*?" How could any sinner ever repent if we told everyone their sins are okay?

Jesus did not die on the cross so we could feel better about ourselves. He died and rose again to save us from ourselves.

To throw stones is wrong.

But to say that sin is okay is also wrong.

Dear friends, this is a very combustible subject. But it's really not that complex. There is certainly a way forward; it's just that many don't like the options:

1. Keep the covenant and let those who disagree go in peace (with land, buildings, and so on).

2. Change the covenant and let those who disagree go in peace.
3. Form a new kind of organizational structure that redefines connection and both sides can live with.
4. Other (perhaps there is some other solution that the Commission will discover).

The Commission has our prayers, as does the called General Conference of 2019. But realistically, what makes us think after all these years that 2019 will settle everything? Will both sides be so satisfied with the results that we expect this decision to stand once and for all? What about 2020 and 2024 and so on?

Let us live together with harmony or separate with graciousness. There is a world watching us. And they aren't just waiting for what we decide. They are watching how we treat one another in the meantime. Together or separate, let's get back to a focus on the Great Commandment and the Great Commission.

4

The Ethics of Love[1]

Magrey R. deVega

Magrey R. DeVega is senior pastor at Hyde Park United Methodist Church, Tampa, Florida.

IN 2018, THE UNITED METHODIST CHURCH will be fifty years old. And it will be in its forty-sixth year debating homosexuality. That is a long time for family members to be at odds.

The dispute has only grown more hostile over recent years, with the church on the precipice of an irreparable split at its most recent General Conference in Portland in May 2016. The election of the first lesbian bishop in July 2016 and the subsequent ruling in April 2017 by the Judicial Council that declared her election a violation of church law have only enflamed the passions on both sides. We continue to pray for the Commission on a Way Forward, a group of thirty-two clergy and laity authorized by the 2016 General Conference to discern a plan for the church to find a way through its current impasse. A specially called General Conference has been set for 2019 in St. Louis, with the express purpose of considering the plan put forward by the Commission.

These are difficult days for a denomination caught in a contentious tug-of-war that feels like there can be no winners.

Not the Church versus Culture, but the Culture of the Church

The argument by some in this debate is that those who have more accepting views of homosexuality have acquiesced to the culture, that we have allowed the ways of the world to shape our belief and practice, rather than the other way around. But to be warm-hearted and open-minded, two of the core values of the local church that I serve, is less about shaping or being shaped by the culture around us. It is about tending to the culture *within* the church. It should be no surprise that many of Paul's letters to the early churches, particularly 1and 2 Corinthians, Ephesians, and Galatians, dealt with the way Christians treated *one another*. And the way we treat one another can itself be a witness to the rest of the world.

So, those like myself who would affirm support for marriage equality and the ordination of gay and lesbian persons, and who would wish to work within our system to make those changes, need to fully embrace and love those who are on the opposite side of the debate. Those with whom we might disagree need to know they are loved, welcomed, and accepted in the church.

Why? Because I recognize that I did not always believe as I do now. Thirty years ago, when I had a very different view of homosexuality, if the United Methodist local church of my youth was condescending of people with a more conservative view, then I would not have felt welcomed there. I likely would have left that church, which means I would not have been called to ministry in that church. I would therefore not be United Methodist today, and I would not be a United Methodist pastor. That is difficult for me to even think about.

This is not to say that I expect others to change their views to be like mine. And it does not mean that if there are those in my local church who agree with me, then I think they are better Christians. Having a church of multiple voices joined together by common mission does not make us weaker or culturally acquiescent.

It makes us multilingual in our mission. And I'm pretty sure that Pentecost would say that's a good thing.

Non-Dualistic Thinking

Besides, if we really wanted to acquiesce to the culture in its present state, then we are doomed to reflect its current polarized, binary, dualistic ways. I cannot help but think of the number of times Jesus was presented with either/or questions. Is it lawful to pay taxes to Caesar or not? Who sinned: this blind man or his parents? Is it right to heal on the Sabbath? Many times, when asked a question about sin posed in the form of a contentious tug-of-war, Jesus refused to play. Not only did he never say a word about homosexuality, he had *a lot more to say* about the grace of God, which transcends either/or categories that are more useful to cast judgment on others than they are in transforming lives.

So, in the church, we must be unafraid to talk about sin. All of us deal with it. None of us are immune to it. We have all fallen short of God's glory. And though many like myself have now come to the place where we believe homosexual persons are created who they are by God, and that living into that identity is not sinful, it does not make that position soft on sin. Because I know of no one, gay or straight, who would claim to be sinless. And it reminds me that the best answer Jesus ever gave to a binary question about sin was this: let the one without sin cast the first stone.

So I'm certain we could all agree on this: we all really need Jesus.

The Ethics of Love

I recognize that some people who do not affirm marriage equality and gay and lesbian ordination say that the central issue is less a question about its sinfulness, and more about preserving traditions and institutions, like marriage and the structures of the church. The concern is that if everyone simply did what they wanted to do, then that would be detrimental to our society. As a rules person myself, I understand this position at a personal level. I do my best to observe covenants and boundaries, and to be obedient to the systems and institutions that govern my life and my calling.

In this light, this part of the debate is a reflection of the larger ongoing tension in the wider culture, among (1) those who value the stability of institutions, (2) those who value the authenticity of personal experience, and (3) those wish to value all perspectives as having equal merit. In terms of Spiral Dynamics, a color-coded theory of human consciousness espoused by psychologist Clare Graves,[2] we are in the midst of a formidable tectonic shift among these three groups, which—put in terms of the Wesleyan Quadrilateral—are those who most value tradition (blue), experience (orange), and reason (green).

This interplay is not new. Within the biblical narrative is an ongoing conversation between the ways of God and the structures of earth. It is a dialogue between God's initiatives and humanity's ways of codifying them. But by the time Jesus came around, he realized that the institutionalization of God's commandments had itself become monolithic, and when faced with the (again, dualistic) question of whether he had come to follow the law or abolish the law, Jesus said neither. He had come to *fulfill* the law.

If there is any bridge to be made among these three polarities in the church, it is the ethics of love. That is the theme that Jesus returned to, time and again, when he was confronted with these questions. For the traditionalist, an ethic of love means that our structures are merely a means to the fulfillment of our mission of sharing God's love. For the experientialist, an ethic of love ought to govern the way we treat one another, even those who don't share in that experience. For the relativist, an ethic of love is the parameter that determines what options are harmful, destructive, and out of bounds.

And for us Christians, there is no greater revelation of that ethic of love than Jesus, revealed to us in the Bible.

The God Who Is Still Speaking

And that is why I believe that God is still speaking to us. Because the times are changing, and the timeless word of God revealed to us in Jesus has the capacity to speak in surprisingly relevant and novel ways. This point is in contrast to one Christian speaker I recently heard, who declared that God is no longer speaking. He claimed that all that God has needed to say to us is revealed to us in the Bible, and that is therefore all we need to know.

One of the singularly transformative moments in my seminary career was in my theology class, where Professor Tyron Inbody said to us, "Okay. Let us accept for a moment that the Bible is the inerrant, infallible word of God, and all that God wishes to say to us about anything is included in it." Then he asked the zinger:

"So what?"

"Isn't it the case," he continued, "that we would still need to interpret it? That we still need to make connections between its words and our times and situations? Of course we do. So, what is to prevent us, as imperfect and mistake-prone as we are, from taking the holy words of God and interpreting them in an unholy way? Every act of interpretation has the capacity for fallibility."

I realized then that he was right. Yes, the Bible is our primary authority. In it is contained all that is necessary for our salvation, in the words of John Wesley. But because we are far from perfect, we need the constant, steady voice of the Holy Spirit to help us interpret the Bible in the way God needs it to be embodied and enlivened in the world today.

The church may have closed the biblical canon. But it did not close the mouth of God.

A Church at the Center

Ultimately, here is why I am energized to be the senior pastor of the local church that I serve, regardless of what is happening in the higher levels of our denomination. The first two of our six core values are that we are a Christ-centered and biblically-rooted church. That is at the core of who we are, and those two values alone define the center of our life together. It is what enables our next two core values, to be both warm-hearted (open to a diversity of people) and open-minded (open to a diversity of perspectives). And because we are mission-directed and connection-committed, we remember that all that we do is guided by an ethic of love.

The world today is governed by a different ethic. It is one of humiliation. It is one where a black teenager cannot walk the neighborhood at night without worrying about being humiliated by a police officer. It is a world where a white male is made to feel humiliated for having too much privilege, when he instead feels so helpless and poor. It is a world where gay and lesbian persons called to ministry feel humiliated by a church that forces them to choose between the way they were created and the way they were called by God. It is a world where a person cannot long for a preservation of tradition without being called a bigot.

But the core values in my local church are clear: humiliation has no place in Christian community. We worship together, debate together, serve together, and love together. Not just because we have more in common than we are different (though we do). And not just because we need one another (and we do).

But because the world needs us. They may not realize it, but they need the institution of the church to be an alternative community against the brokenness of the world. It is a community not shaped by the polarizing dynamics of our society, but by an ethic of love. And because there are way too many people in the world who need Jesus, and we are the body of Christ.

Now, more than ever, it is good to be the church. And we must strive to make God's love real together.

NOTES

1. First published in *Hyde Park UMC News*, May 11, 2017, "All News, Midweek Message, Top News"— http://hydeparkumc.org/midweek-message-broad-center-church/#. Accessed November 13, 2017.
2. Clare Graves, "Colors of Thinking," http://www.spiraldynamics.ua/Graves/colors.htm. Accessed November 13, 2017.

5

"Upright of Heart": A Wesleyan Reflection on Diversity and Division

David N. Field

David N. Field is academic coordinator of the Methodist e-Academy, Basel, Switzerland.

THE UNITED METHODIST CHURCH wrestles with the threat posed to its continued existence by the ferment resulting from diverse and contradictory theological and ethical positions. Debates have become conflicts, with people and congregations taking strongly adversarial sides. Some form of separation seems inevitable. However late the hour, I believe that John Wesley's theology provides significant insights that point the way to a more reconciled future.[1]

One potentially fruitful approach is suggested by Wesley's comments on 1 Corinthians 11:19 in the *Explanatory Notes upon the New Testament.* Wesley writes: "God permits them [divisions], that it might appear among you who are, and who are not, upright of heart."[2] Wesley uses the phrase "upright of heart" in a number of places where he is discussing diversity of theological positions and the tensions caused by divergence and contradiction in theological positions. In the preface to his edition of Clarke's *Lives of Eminent Persons* he states:

> . . . the same Spirit works the same work of grace in men upright in heart, of whatever denomination. These, how widely soever they differ in opinion,

> all agree in one mind, one temper. How far distant they are from each other with regard to the circumstances of worship, they all meet in the substance of true worship, 'the faith that worketh by love.'[3]

Taken together, these two passages offer a potentially fruitful perspective on how we should approach the reality of theological diversity and contradiction within Christian communities. Diversity and division provide a context in which uprightness of heart can be manifested, but this uprightness of heart is not identified with a particular theological position. Rather, it is compatible with a variety of theological positions and is a point of unity in the midst of diversity. In this article I will briefly explore what Wesley means by the phrase "upright of heart" and then suggest some ways in which it can contribute to reshaping our approach to diversity and division.

Upright of Heart

Wesley uses this phrase a number of times in his writings and assumes that readers will know what he means, but he never actually defines it. For Wesley the heart was the center of our personality that motivates our outward life; it combines settled attitudes, entrenched emotions, characteristic ways of thinking, deeply held values, and typical responses to God, others, and the world.[4] If the heart is upright it has integrity; it is genuine in its relation to God. Thus Wesley associates an upright heart with honesty, undivided commitment, a good conscience, a unity of genuine motive and action in worship and giving, seeking to please God, and the desire to conform to God's will. An upright heart was the product of God's grace in the life of a person. Wesley recognized that there were degrees of uprightness: a person responding to prevenient grace and genuinely seeking God was to a degree upright in heart, a person who had experienced the new birth was to a greater extent upright in heart before God, and sanctification culminating in Christian perfection led to greater levels of uprightness. When related to other aspects of Wesley's theology, it can be argued that to be "upright of heart" is to live in a genuine transforming relationship with God in which one's outward life matches the motivations of one's heart; that is, they give expression to a genuine love for God and our fellow human beings.

"Upright of Heart" and Theological Disagreement

Returning to Wesley's comments on 1 Corinthians 11:19, Wesley is proposing that situations of disagreement and division in the church provide a unique context in which the genuineness of people's relationship to God is manifested. How we respond to conflict demonstrates the condition of our hearts. Importantly, uprightness of heart is not identified with a particular set of theological propositions. Hence God does not allow conflicts in order to demonstrate which theological position is right, but which hearts are upright. Thus, as we approach such situations of disagreement and diversity, the ultimate goal is not to win the argument or to prove that our position is true—but rather to give expression to the transformation the Holy Spirit is working in our lives so that we love God and love our neighbors and, in this case, particularly our fellow Christians with whom God has called us to relationships of mutual love and delight. What form, then, does this manifestation take?

Uprightness of Heart and Theological Conviction

The emphasis that being upright of heart is compatible with a diversity of theological positions does not mean that it is compatible with theological indifference. In his classic sermon "Catholic Spirit," Wesley strongly rejected "latitudinarianism"—the treating of theological positions and disagreements as matters of indifference.[5] Uprightness of heart recognizes that theological and ethical differences are significant and can have serious consequences. In our present context, the debate around LGBTQ inclusion has serious consequences. If the conservative position is correct, then those arguing for the affirmation of same-sex relationships are advocating sinful practices that are contrary to God's purpose for sexuality, are contrary to people's holistic well-being, and have serious spiritual consequences. If those who advocate an affirming position are right, then those advocating a conservative position are advocating a position that is counter to the overarching message of the Bible, is driving people away from the gospel, and is psychologically harmful. Being upright of heart requires us to acknowledge the reality and seriousness of the differences, but to find a way to deal with them that manifests a heart transformed by God's grace.

Uprightness of Heart and Freedom of Conscience

In "Catholic Spirit" Wesley relates being upright of heart to having "a conscience void of offence."[6] He goes on to stress the importance of following the dictates of your own conscience and not compelling others to accept your opinions or follow your practices. The reason Wesley gives for this is that all human beings are responsible before God for their opinions and actions. As such they ought to believe and act on the basis of what they are genuinely convinced before God is true and correct. Wesley recognized that a person's conscience is influenced by numerous factors but insisted that people "must not act contrary to their conscience even if it is an erroneous one."[7] He thus insisted that all people have "liberty to choose our own religion, to worship God according to our own conscience according to the best light we have."[8] Freedom of conscience has significance within the church; Wesley argued that his preachers should only obey bishops and follow the church laws to the extent that they could with a "safe conscience."[9] Being upright of heart requires one to accept the good consciences of others even when one disagrees with them. This does not mean one ignores the differences, especially if one is convinced that they are spiritually harmful. In such a context one has the responsibility before God to inform and reason with others, seeking to convince them of their mistake. At the same time they have a responsibility before God to do the same.

Uprightness of Heart and the Evaluation of the Hearts of Others

Wesley was well aware that in his day—as in ours—theological debate moves quickly from debate about issues to denigration of one's opponents and their motives. In contrast he argued that love requires us to think better of others than ourselves. Uprightness of heart entails an honest evaluation of our own motives, desires, and goals as we engage in theological dispute and a deep awareness of the way we easily deceive ourselves with recognition that sin cleaves to our best deeds and motives.[10] The result of this is that people of upright heart will always be more rigorous in evaluating themselves and aware of their wrong motives and will always seek to put the best interpretation on the motives, desires, and goals of those they disagree with. As Wesley notes, "every one knows more evil of himself than he can of another."[11] He goes as far as to argue that a genuine love for those one disagrees with should lead one to defend their characters.[12] How far we have come from the Wesleyan ideal: the social media, blogs, and even the communications of various caucus groups are quick to judge the character and motives of those they disagree with. Those who hold a conservative view of marriage and sexuality are quickly labeled bigoted and hateful. Those who affirm same-sex marriage are labeled as underhanded, deceptive, and disruptive. This is not to deny that this characterization might be true in some cases, but rather to affirm that it is not always the case. Progress in living together depends on mutual respect, even when there is disagreement.

Separation, Schism, and Uprightness of Heart

The context of Wesley's comments that "God permits them [divisions], that it might appear among you who are, and who are not, upright of heart" is Paul's response to divisions within the church at Corinth. Commenting on this, Wesley makes a distinction between "schism" as described in the text and separation. Wesley argues that for Paul "schism" refers to "uncharitable divisions" within the church that are the consequence of a lack of genuine love for one another, and "heresies" refer to the "outward divisions or parties" that result from the uncharitable divisions.[13] What is ultimately divisive is not the difference of theological positions, but the lack of genuine love that results in these differences leading to conflict and divisions with all their negative consequences. For Wesley, the significant issue is not merely the structural separation of Christians but the host of unloving attitudes, words, and actions that accompany such divisions. These embody not a spirit of love but one of hatred. When a church embodies such a spirit in its life, it is denying its identity and mission as the community called to embody God's love in the world. The manifestation of being upright of heart emerges in contrast to the situation of division and conflict. The genuinely upright of heart will be manifested by their offering an alternative way of dealing with theological difference and contradiction.

In his later sermon "On Schism," Wesley reaffirms his understanding of schism but goes on to address the subject of separation from a church. He states:

> To separate ourselves from a body of living Christians, with whom we were before united, is a grievous breach of the law of love. It is the nature of love to unite us together, and the greater the love, the stricter the union. And while this continues in its strength, nothing can divide those whom love has united. It is only when our love grows cold that we can think of separating from our brethren. And this is certainly the case with any who willingly separate from their Christian brethren. The pretenses for separation may be innumerable, but want of love is always the real cause; otherwise they would still hold the unity of the spirit in the bond of peace.[14]

Wesley goes on to specify that in certain conditions, separation would be legitimate. These are when one could not remain without being forced to act against one's conscience either by being compelled to do something that one is convinced is contrary to the will of God or by being prevented from doing something one is convinced is the will of God. Wesley proposes that in these cases the fault lies with those who prevent one from acting in accordance with one's conscience. While it is clear that the church must have boundaries, if we take Wesley seriously then love requires that the church should structure itself so as to allow for people to have as much freedom as possible to act in accordance with their conscience. In other writings, Wesley's argument that Methodists should remain within the Church of England suggests another reason why separation is contrary to love. He argued that Methodism was raised up to be a renewal movement within the Church of England and to withdraw was to reject this calling.[15] It could thus be argued that love requires one to remain within a church in order to be an agent of renewal. Writing toward the end of his life when Methodism was making progress within the Church of England, he stated, "It would be contrary to all common sense as well as good conscience to make a separation now."[16] In the context of debate over the possibility of separation from the church or of compelling others to separate, an upright heart can be manifested in two complementary ways. The first is in working for the maintenance of the unity of the church in such a way that enables people to live and serve in accordance with their conscience. The second is by remaining, despite difficulties, in order to promote the renewal of the church. This is, however, not to denigrate the integrity of those who in good conscience cannot remain in a denomination that, for example, ordains openly gay and lesbian people. Such people are also manifesting an upright heart when they are genuinely acting in accordance with their conscience even if, from my perspective, there is no necessity for separation in light of Wesley's understanding of the church.

Concluding Reflections on The UMC and the Upright Heart

The theological diversity that has characterized United Methodism has provided an opportunity for the manifestation of communities of people with upright hearts who lived in relationship with one another despite their diversity of theological position. Sadly, the present crisis is in many cases the demonstration that we have failed to do this. It is easy to lay the blame on one group or another. I would suggest that the way of an upright heart is to recognize our common participation in this failure. Not because of the positions we advocated in good conscience were necessarily wrong, but because of the way we have participated in the spiral of party spirit, division, and a lack of love. Hence the starting point for the way ahead is not firstly structural but spiritual. It must begin with honest self-examination that seeks to uncover the sin that cleaves to our best motives and actions. Such self-examination must lead to repentance for sin. Repentance should be accompanied by lament for the brokenness and pain caused by sin. Repentance and lament can open a path to reconciliation in the midst of diverse and even contradictory positions. Such reconciliation in a Wesleyan Spirit could be given liturgical form in a renewal of our covenant with God and our siblings in Christ.

NOTES

1. My book *Bid Our Jarring Conflicts Cease: A Wesleyan Theology and Praxis of Church Unity* (Nashville: Foundery Books, 2017) is an attempt to provide an in-depth exploration of important aspects of Wesley's theology in this regard. The present article, however, approaches this from another angle.
2. John Wesley, *Explanatory Notes upon the New Testament* (Bristol: Graham and Pine, 1760-62; repr. London: Epworth, 1976).
3. "Preface to Clarke's *Lives of Eminent Persons.* §4 in *Works (Jackson)*, 14:232.
4. See the discussion in *Bid Our Jarring Conflicts Cease* 2 and the references there to other literature.
5. See Sermon 39 "Catholic Spirit" §3:1, in John Wesley, *The Works of John Wesley,* The Bicentennial Edition (Nashville: Abingdon Press), 2:92 & 93.
6. Sermon 39 "Catholic Spirit" §1:8, *The Works of John Wesley,* 2:85.
7. *Journal* of June 3, 1776, *The Works of John Wesley,* 23:20.
8. *Thoughts upon Liberty* §16, in John Wesley, *The Works of the Rev. John Wesley, M.A.,* ed. Thomas Jackson, 3rd ed., 14 vols. (London: Wesleyan Methodist Book Room, 1872; reprinted Grand Rapids: Baker Book House, 1979), 11: 37.

9. "Minutes of The London Conference of June 25-29, 1744," Monday, June 24th, §52, *Works of Wesley,* 10:135.
10. See Sermon 14 "The Repentance of Believers" §§1:11-13, *The Works of John Wesley* 1:341–343.
11. *Explanatory Notes upon the New Testament,* Phil 2:3; see also his notes on Mark 9:40 and his discussion of love in Sermon 22 "Upon Our Lord's Sermon on the Mount II §§3:15 & 16, *The Works of John Wesley,* 1:506.
12. Sermon 38 "A Caution Against Bigotry" §4:5, *The Works of John Wesley,* 2:77.
13. *Notes upon the New Testament* 1 Cor. 11:18.
14. Sermon 75 "On Schism" §2:11, *The Works of John Wesley,* 3:64.
15. See "Reasons Against a Separation from the Church of England," *The Works of John Wesley,* 9:334–341.
16. Letter to Samuel Bardsley, March 25, 1787 in *The Letters of John Wesley,* ed. John Telford, (London: Epworth, 1931), 7:377.

6

Multiply or Divide?

Rob Fuquay

Rob Fuquay is senior pastor of St. Luke's United Methodist Church, Indianapolis.

"EITHER WE BELIEVE IN absolute truth or not."

The woman who said that to me learned her husband was leaving her. She wanted me to "preach" to him and use the authority of Scripture to compel him to be a responsible Christian man and return home. After all, the Bible is clear, God hates divorce. Never mind that she didn't want to hear his reasons for leaving. It was time to pull the "absolute truth" card and appeal to any shred of religious responsibility he might have left. Desperate times call for desperate measures, right?

Well, it's a desperate time in our United Methodist Church. We are facing the real possibility of divide over an issue some see as a clear matter of absolute truth: whether LGBTQ persons should be granted full admission in the church, including the right to be married in our churches, serve in leadership, and be ordained. The trouble with absolute truth is there can be uncertainty over what is absolute. Many people see it as an absolute truth that all races are equal. Yet the rise of hate groups would say not everyone agrees. Many believe it is an absolute truth that women have the right to serve at any level of leadership in the church. Yet there are many Christian groups who vehemently disagree. Some say it is an absolute truth that divorced people should be expelled from the church and not allowed in leadership. How's your church doing with that one?

If a truth is so absolute, then why isn't it clear to all people? Maybe the responsibility doesn't lie so much with God as with us. As Wesleyan Christians, we affirm the role of free choice. Human beings are not automatons. We can accept God's will or go our own way. This freedom can take us closer to God or away from God. God's will is intimately linked to the freedom God gives us.

Since absolute truths are not written in the sky, we have to use our fundamental, theological right and gift as human beings to decide what is truth, what is okay to compromise, and what should never be compromised. This is where our Wesleyan tradition offers a great deal of help in our approach to Scripture, our understanding of grace, our passion for the nature and mission of the church, and our value for Christian community. Let me show you what I mean.

I am the pastor of St. Luke's United Methodist Church in Indianapolis. Our mission statement reads: *We are an open community of Christians helping people find and give hope through Jesus Christ.* The words *open community* are very important in the life of this church. We are committed to making disciples in the context of a community that welcomes all people: black, white, Asian, refugee, gay, straight, rich, poor, and all other labels that comprise the diversity of God's children.

But be careful about putting a label on us like "liberal." We run the political gamut at St. Luke's. We have extreme conservatives and ultra-progressives. If I say something in a sermon that hints of a political slant left or right, then I hear it from both sides. Hoosiers tend to get passionate about their politics! Yet the unifying element of this community of believers is being open to everyone. We talk about being a "big tent" with lots of opinions. Our differences are many, but our passion is for helping all people find hope through Jesus Christ and becoming a part of God's hope-giving mission in the world. We are not fighting over who should be in or out. We are not divided over issues like same-sex marriage. We have some who would prefer that a definition of marriage remain between one man and one woman. We have some who feel it is time to leave The United Methodist Church because we don't grant rights to same-gender couples as accorded by our nation. But the ethos of this church is to work it out *together*. At the end of the day, we believe unity should prevail over differences, provided that unity is grounded in the love of God in Jesus Christ.

Writing this article has given me cause to reflect on what makes the diversity of St. Luke's work. I believe a number of Wesleyan values are the reason.

Taking a High View of Scripture

We approach the Bible the way John Wesley did. He said he was "a man of one book," which didn't mean the Bible was the only book he read. He was a brilliant scholar, but the Bible was the primary source for understanding God's truth. This is why the label *quadrilateral* is really a misnomer for describing Wesley's four primary sources for decision-making: Scripture, tradition, reason, and experience. They were not four equal parts for Wesley, but more like a three-legged stool with Scripture as the seat standing over the other three.

The Bible for Wesley was the single most important means of grace for understanding the character and nature of God, how we should live, and directions for getting to heaven. Yet this didn't make Wesley a literalist. Our *Book of Discipline* captures the Wesleyan tradition of biblical interpretation in saying "scripture is the inspired word of God." Not literal. Not inerrant. But inspired. God spoke to and through fallible human beings. Do Wesleyan Christians get unhinged by the idea that there could be errors in the Bible? Not at all. God is the One who is perfect, not anything or anyone else. We don't worship the Bible; we worship God and understand God's truth most perfectly in the life of Jesus Christ.

Therefore we have room for interpretation. We even see this tension over reinterpreting the Bible in the Bible! Consider Acts 15.

The first church conference was held in Jerusalem to decide whether Gentiles should obey all of the Torah's requirements for holy living. At the end of the day they decided some laws need to remain while others did not, based on new revelations and experiences of God. In other words, they made choices. They took what Scripture said, what they knew at the time, their own experiences, and they allowed for something that previously was unbiblical. As a result, unity in the church prevailed and the mission increased.

So let's consider this approach with Scriptures dealing with same-sex relations. On one side people say the Bible is clear: any sexual activity outside of a marriage relationship between a man and a woman is a sin. That settles it. Others on this side argue that Christians who are not heterosexual just need to remain celibate in order to be faithful.

On the other side people look at the way we have reinterpreted the Bible's treatment of slavery, rights of women, and even divorce as a model for how we need to understand verses dealing with same-sex attraction. The Bible might be clear, but that doesn't mean it should be binding for all time. The Old Testament commanded stoning a rebellious child to death. But what qualifies as rebellious? And even if we believed this today, what do we do with the parable of the Prodigal Son? Jesus also said a rich man cannot enter the kingdom of God. But what does it mean to be rich? Does our net assets value determine whether we get into heaven? Are these absolute truths? Or do they need interpretation in the light of tradition, reason, and experience?

The stalemate over biblical interpretation has defined our approach, but what if the Bible holds the key for a way forward? What if we practiced the pattern of Acts 15? What if leading voices on both sides came together with the primary goal of seeking to maintain unity in the church as the leaders in Jerusalem did? What if we didn't demand one way or the other but allowed orthodox and progressive views to be kept? What could *that* church look like? What if our first priority was to create a church that is open to all who desire to be devoted followers of Jesus Christ?

The Nature of Grace

I remember sitting with Bishop Dick Wills when he was pastor of Christ UMC in Ft. Lauderdale. He told about meeting with the mother of one of his members about the United Methodist understanding of baptism. The woman's grandchild was to be baptized, but she didn't believe in infant baptism. For her it was a matter of absolute truth. Dr. Wills gave it his best shot, but each approach was met with quick rebuttals and scripture quoting.

Exasperated, Dr. Wills finally said, "I don't claim to be right. At the end of the day I believe that if I err I err on the side of grace. It's important to your daughter that you be there for your grandchild's baptism. Will you err on the side of grace?" The Sunday came, the couple brought their child forward for baptism, and in the congregation the grandmother's seat remained empty.

Grace is at the heart of our Wesleyan theology. This is our absolute truth. This is what we should turn to in our differences, a willingness to err on the side of grace. One day we will give an account to God for the church we left behind, and it is hard to see the wrong in granting full acceptance to people who live by Wesley's three rules—do no harm, do good, and stay in love with God. Even if our conscience doesn't allow us to take that position, perhaps we can be in a "big tent" and remain in a church that allows for others who do.

Wesley once preached a sermon titled *The Catholic Spirit.* Using a passage from 2 Kings 10:15, he addressed how Christians should handle differences of opinion. He recommended these questions for our opponents: Is your heart right with God? Do you believe in the Lord Jesus Christ? Is your faith filled with the energy of love? Is your heart right toward your neighbor? Do you show good works? (Perhaps Wesley was recommending these as absolutes truths?) Once affirmed, Wesley says, "Give me your hand," and then explains:

> I do not mean, "Be of my opinion." You need not. I do not expect or desire it. Neither do I mean, "I will be of your opinion." I cannot, it does not depend on my choice. I can no more think, than I can see or hear, as I will. Keep you your opinion; I mine; and that as steadily as ever. You need not even endeavour to come over to me, or bring me over to you. I do not desire you to dispute those points, or to hear or speak one word concerning them. Let all opinions alone on one side and the other: only "give me thine hand."[1]

What if we just show grace to one another and assume we all want to see people brought to Christ, grow in their faith, and transform the world? What if we just give each other a hand?

Preserving the Mission of the Church

Some years ago I served a church that divided over a decision to convert our old sanctuary into a youth building. The deeper emotions for some had to do with the rapid growth of the congregation that made them feel left out.

This group called for a church conference. We met with the district superintendent beforehand, and he said it was his goal to preserve unity no matter what. I respectfully disagreed. I suggested that unity around the wrong thing is not good over time. I asked that he might lead us in seeking unity around our mission and the power of being of one heart for the sake of the gospel.

He did a great job leading a meeting that, while filled with tension, provided wonderful statements of faith and affirmation for our mission. Our vote was far from unanimous; but we affirmed the trustees' decision, and over the following six years the church experienced great growth and a strong sense of unity.

What if we approached our current divide in United Methodism not as a right or a wrong, but as an opportunity to expand our mission? What if we gave room for all sides of the debate to coexist as one church and welcome the chance to reach more people for Christ? What if this potential schism has arrived not to divide us but to help us multiply? I am privileged to serve a church much like every congregation in my ministry, where we have people on the extreme left and right who love Jesus and live together in the same family of God. What if our denomination lived like the local church?

Christian Community

Finally, consider the value of authentic Christian community. I say to our new member classes, as a way of encouraging people to join small groups, that there is no concept of Christian faith in the New Testament apart from community. We grow closer to Christ through fellowship with other believers.

Wesley advocated the practice of "Christian conferencing." This was not a meeting! Conferencing was about joining other Christians for mutual encouragement and dialogue. Such conferencing was critical not only for individual health but for the health of the body of Christ. As we listen for God speaking through one another, and not just through those who hold our opinion, we learn and discern God's will for us personally and corporately.

I have watched this play out over and over in the church I serve. When racial tensions rise in our city, we participate in dialogues with people of other races to learn and grow. When debates over immigration heat up, we provide forums to hear refugees share about their experience. When Indiana became a major test state prior to the Supreme Court's decision affirming marriage equality, we provided studies such as *The Bible Tells Me So,* to hear faithful Christians wrestle with what the Bible says about homosexuality. Does this mean everyone's opinion changed? No. It does help people experience respect for their opinion, and I believe it is a big reason why our diversity is a strength.

Either we believe in absolute truth or not. It is a good point. It makes for a great conversation in the church, the kind I believe they had in Acts 15. For centuries the church has found agreement in declaring belief in the love and power of our Creator God; the grace of Jesus Christ; the power of the Holy Spirit; the forgiveness of sin; the resurrection hope of Jesus Christ; the communion of saints; and life everlasting. As for debates on nonessentials, Wesley's advice is to "think and let think."

Can we keep The United Methodist Church together with such differences of opinion? I'd like to believe so, because I experience the possibility every day. I get to be a part of a church that holds the tensions together. What if our denomination could work this out like the local church does?

Many years ago I served a congregation with two interesting members. One was a founder of the Good News movement. The other a retired district superintendent who identified himself as a "yellow dog democrat," which was a description of his theology as much as his politics. These two men shared little in common except for a devotion to Jesus Christ. A year or so after moving from that church I got a letter from the conservative member. He sent me a copy of his funeral service. He had planned it out and wanted me to be available in case his current pastor was not. He had many people participating in the service. One of them was the old yellow dog! Why? Because these two men had a friendship and deep respect for each other that superseded their differences. They chose to focus on what united them rather than what divided them.

If the local church is big enough for such diversity, then certainly our denomination is.

NOTES

1. John Wesley, "Catholic Spirit," Sermon 39, II.1, Wesley Center Online, http://wesley.nnu.edu/john-wesley/the-sermons-of-john-wesley-1872-edition/sermon-39-catholic-spirit/. Accessed November 14, 2017.

7

Love's Competing Demands

Diane Kenaston

Diane Kenaston is pastor of University United Methodist Church in St. Louis.

MY KNEES SHOOK AS I faced the congregation. I breathed quickly and shallowly in the few seconds I had to decide what to do. Slowly, I took the microphone. The Scout leader—I'll call her Gladys—had said her piece. She had thanked the Boy Scouts and their families for filling our lovely country church to capacity on this Scout Sunday. They had smiled back at her, glowing in her praise. It was easy to see why Gladys was a beloved saint of the church. She was the kind of woman who calmed preschoolers, visited the sick, crocheted prayer shawls, fed the trustees, arranged for behind-the-scenes camp scholarships, and corralled elementary school boys and their families into Scouting. When these boys grew up and became young men and Eagle Scouts, they credited Gladys's persistent sainthood. It was a testament to their love of Gladys that led the boys and their families to crowd the pews on this day.

Then Gladys concluded her praise of the boys with a fervent prayer request: "Please pray for the Scouts. At National they are talking about letting homosexuals in. And I just can't — I just can't imagine putting my boys in a tent with one of them." Her voice caught in her throat.

What she could not imagine, I could. I imagined a Boy Scout lying awake after his tent mates fell asleep, replaying the words he heard in worship, convinced that God and all the saints of the church were allied against him. I imagined him trying to figure out how to earn God's love like a badge. I imagined him concluding that since his very existence horrified his Scout leader, he could not be honest or brave. Instead, he needed to hide his truth from everyone, including himself.

As I stood in the trembling silence, there was no way forward. I could not show equal love to gay Scouts and scared saints at the same time. Speaking the truth in love would cut like a sword. If I stayed silent, I could avoid shattering the congregation's earnest assumption that all true Christians draw boundaries the same way they do. I would preserve the carefully built unity of a vocally conservative congregation and their secretly progressive pastor. But my silence would mean that my instinct for self-preservation outweighed my love for our neighbors. Love demanded the sacrifice of unity.

"We will pray for the Boy Scouts as they make this decision. As we do so, let me share official United Methodist teaching," I faltered. "Our church teaches that all people are created in the image of God and are beloved by God. We welcome all people, including gays and lesbians, into lay leadership in the church. Every individual is a person of sacred worth."

People shifted uncomfortably in their seats. Were they exchanging glances? Was I imagining things? Was that person walking to the bathroom—or walking out? Was Gladys hurt? Would she try to take the mic back?

My courage lasted only as long as my shaking voice did. All afternoon I waited for a call from the district superintendent. But the phone was silent. No one mentioned what had happened. Is silence a sign of love? Does avoiding conflict mean we are living the gospel? I walked on tiptoes for a week before I started breathing normally again. From the vantage point of five years later, perhaps my fears were unfounded. I know preachers who have been driven out of churches for less—but my statement seemed especially small and measly. Why should a simple summary of church teaching cause a fuss? Maybe love can hold a church together in unity.

So I focused on loving. I preached. I visited. I thanked Gladys at each potluck for the beautiful table decorations. "We're called to share the good news of God's love," I preached. But when charge conference reviewed the list of inactive members, one of the older saints of the church whispered to me,

"That couple left years ago because their son came out as gay—and they didn't want anyone to know." They had left the church because they had known that their close-knit family of faith would not be willing to extend God's love to their whole family. Although I wrote letters and left messages asking if I could visit, the family never responded. I never got to share one-on-one that I could help them find a church that would welcome them.

"We're only as sick as our secrets," I would say on pastoral calls. But the silence around human sexuality was too toxic to touch. My self-enforced code was that of ecclesial unity. So I refused to publicly proclaim or push for anything greater than "Christians have different opinions on this." The whispers (did I imagine them?) were nauseating.

Then we had another family leave the church. This family left because they got into a fight with their small group: was homosexuality a worse sin than any other sin? The people who stayed were adamant that while homosexuality was a sin, all sins were equal. The people who left were horrified; they believed that homosexuality had to be a worse sin than their own family's divorces.

I was so frustrated. I had compromised my own integrity to live in fear and silence. And still, people were leaving. Even as we failed to love and welcome people of all sexual orientations and gender identities/expressions, we were also failing to love one another. My silence had not bought unity. This realization led me to feel conflicted over my desire for no conflict. If I, as a preacher, was inauthentic, how could we cultivate authentic community? If we were afraid of pushback and division, how would we follow Jesus to the cross?

Following Jesus means facing our fears. I confess that my own fear of rejection and my anxiety over open conflict have kept me from speaking true words of love, even when those words could free and liberate. I have cared too much about laying my head each night in a parsonage, and I have not cared enough about following the One who had nowhere to lay his head. Jesus knew the cost of love, and he was willing to sacrifice his security and his community for that love. Jesus was unafraid to lose everything. When the time came, Jesus even sacrificed his community. Leaving his religious followers, he died among those excluded from traditional piety.

In seminary, I once asked an older, left-leaning, centrist clergyman where he would go if the denomination split. "Diane," he sagely intoned, "you go where your pension goes." I made fun of that response for years. Prophets and profits are homophonous opposites. One rarely leads to the other. Mid-century profits led to bigger barns and Christian education buildings we can no longer fill, much less pay to re-roof. Prophets, on the other hand, imitate Elisha; they are more likely to sic a bear on someone than ride a bull market. I always wanted to be a prophet—right up until I risked being rejected. Then I had no bears to maul detractors, and the statement about protecting clergy pensions didn't seem so funny anymore. When we are concerned about protecting what we have, we bury the gifts of God. We play it safe, and what little we have will be taken from us.

Perhaps Jesus is calling us to empty ourselves of all but love. Like the rich young ruler, we shake our heads in sadness at the cost of Jesus' call. We have so much when we are united as a denomination. With our disaster relief and mission giving, we make a difference in far-flung communities in crisis. With our Social Principles and Resolutions, we advocate in the halls of power. We sing music that unites us across both time and space. Our curriculum, scholarships, and historical archives pass on our accumulated wisdom. We send the next generation to summer camps and then seminaries. We are one of the only remaining mainline denominations to advocate for women and racial-ethnic minorities through agencies dedicated to that purpose. When we hear God's call to sell all we have, to deny ourselves and follow, we know that we will not only give up our apportionments and our trademarked cross-and-flame logo. We will lose our connection. How will we answer the question, "And are we yet alive?"

So we walk away, trembling, knowing that there is no way forward that does not involve great loss. Surely, there must be another way! Decline, decay, and obsolescence are manifestations of that great enemy, Death. So we look at statistics and call them "vital signs." We commission a report and draw an electrocardiogram on the front. We give ourselves prescriptions and argue over the diagnosis. Every specialist offers a different explanation, a different prognosis. We just need to try harder. We can avoid denominational death. We can stay united. We can save ourselves from ourselves.

Our denomination has been fighting for longer than I have been alive over the full inclusion of lesbian, gay, bisexual, transgender, queer, intersex, and asexual (LGBTQIA+) persons in The United Methodist Church. As we prepare for General Conference 2019, we are urged to ask, "How might United Methodists bear witness to graceful and mutually respectful ways of living in the Wesleyan tradition amid enduring disagreements?" This is the wrong question. Better questions ask, "As followers of Jesus, how do we love as Christ first loved us? How do we bear witness to God's love? Are we going on to perfection in love?"

Jesus never asked the disciples to vote on whether he should set his face toward Jerusalem. There was no road except the *via dolorosa*. To try to find another way was a desire driven by anxiety and fear rather than by trust and love. The disciples' lack of love became clear when a "sinful" woman anointed Jesus' feet: Judas had already prepared the report on global financial implications.

Loving our neighbor demands more of us than trying to protect the denomination. Love chooses to be vulnerable. Love does not know the precise steps forward. Rather, the Spirit empowers us to follow Christ in downward mobility through radical, self-giving love.

We are caught in The United Methodist Church with competing demands of love: will we love our neighbors or love our enemies? God calls us to the love that breaks every chain. In love, we die to ourselves. In love, captives go free. In love, the poor are lifted up and the rich go away empty. Love chooses to side with those who are vulnerable and hurting. Trying to love without division reflects the vain belief that avoiding conflict is the same as following Christ. When we refuse to choose sides, we have still, *de facto*, chosen: we are upholding the powerful and privileged by supporting the status quo. To not choose sides is to ally against the God of the oppressed. God calls us, instead, to the love that chooses sides.

I choose to love the people most harmed by our current denominational policies. I will show my love for people of every sexual orientation and gender expression or identity. My love for them leads me to hate the sin of homophobia. I try to "hate the sin, love the sinner," but that distinction is not possible for me. I struggle to love the people caught in the smog of this social sin. I confess that I can rattle off too quickly the names of people and groups in The United Methodist Church who I see as my enemies. I have little doubt that they could do the same, naming people and groups I most dearly love.

At General Conference, we locate our enemies inside of the church. Our fears are personified in one another. So how do we answer God's call to love our enemies? Is it even possible to do so while acting in loving solidarity with those who are most oppressed by those enemies? It is indeed problematic to see our enemies as other people within the church. Even more problematic is when those outside of the church understand the church's exclusion to mean that they and their loved ones are enemies of God.

So on that Scout Sunday, legs trembling, in my own small way, I risked making enemies of my own in order to prevent a child from perceiving that he was God's enemy. The lack of response from that day made me wonder whether I did enough. When the history books are written about this church era, the small acts of truth-telling, of taking a side in love, might be viewed as too slow and too timid. Eighty years ago, my great-grandfather helped to host the 1939 Uniting Conference in Missouri. I have always been slightly ashamed that he stood by as the new Methodist denomination sanctioned segregation and rolled back clergy rights for women. As I prepare to help host the 2019 General Conference—again in Missouri—I worry about what my great-grandchildren will think. Will they judge me complicit in sacrificing beautiful queer saints on the altar of unity? Will our love of the current church prevent us from loving the church as it could be?

You see, I loved Gladys. My fear in speaking that day was not just a love of my own guaranteed appointment. My fear was deeper: it was that love wouldn't sustain us if we told the truth. I believed that love for one group inevitably created enemies of another.

When I got the news that Gladys had died, I wept. She was a beloved child of God, beautiful to behold. By that time, I was in a new church, a new city, a new conference. In this new setting, I did not have to be prophetic, only pastoral. I no longer felt the pressure to hide in public and love behind the scenes. I did not have to pretend unity in order to keep a flock together. I could just love people exactly as they were—and trust that they could love me, too.

One of these new congregants was a man I will call Pete. With his original family, Pete had come out and gotten thrown out. He became homeless in two senses of the word: unhoused and without a family to call "home." He spent time in various churches, but each time he fled before they could get to know him—the real him.

We met Pete at our city's Pridefest. He couldn't believe there were churches there. We told him, "You are a beloved child of God." We heard his story and echoed back to him all of the gifts we see: "You are made in God's image. You have sacred worth." We helped Pete move from a communal living environment into an apartment on his own.

Pete was baptized on All Saints Sunday. "We're all saints," we repeated. We don't have to earn the status of "beloved saint" through doing a long list of good deeds for the local church. We become saints simply by living in the grace of a crucified and risen Christ. We are made holy through love.

Before his baptism, Pete gave a testimony. "I always knew that I was a gay man who loved God. But before coming here, I could never imagine—" he stopped, his voice caught in his throat. "I never imagined that God could possibly love me, too."

Neither Gladys nor Pete could imagine a gay man being loved by God. Like a Scout, God's love is brave and trustworthy. God's love gives us the courage to be authentic and real. God calls us to a future greater than we can imagine.

Someday, Gladys and Pete will meet. That future feels unimaginable.

To prepare for that faraway someday, did they need to be part of the same denomination here and now? I don't know. I love them both. I see their gifts and their flaws. I know I'm equally gifted and flawed, and I don't have all of the answers in terms of polity, or what the church "should" do.

What I do know is that one of these days, we are going to stand, legs shaking, before Jesus. We will be there with all the saints of the church—both the ones who thought that they earned that title and those who were convinced that they were God's enemies. The area before God's throne will be filled to capacity—all of us saying, "I always thought I loved God. I just never really imagined how much God could possibly love me." We'll turn, trembling, to see all of those we would have excluded: "I never imagined how much God could possibly love you too."

On that day, the Spirit will put to death our present despair. We will see the rising of an unimagined future. Christ will hold out his hands, bearing the scars of the ecclesial body as he invites us to be remade in the Triune image, made one as God is One.

The way to which Jesus beckons us forward is the way of the cross. We are called to humbly and lovingly submit ourselves to the cruciform life. When we are willing to die to ourselves, we will be united with the excluded and rejected of our world. There we will encounter love in all love's vulnerability and fullness. Our fear of dying is a sign that we are not yet perfected in this love; for perfect love casts out fear.

This call to the cross is for all of us. Straight cis people like me have spent several decades praying, "Lord, let this cup pass from me." But we cannot avoid the cup. It is the cup of sacrifice that we have required LGBTQIA+ United Methodists to drink over and over. Their love for the church, love for neighbor, love for God, and, yes, even love for enemies, has been shown in the bleeding cup and broken body. Their brave proclamation of truth breaks our silence and challenges us to greater love. No one has greater love than this: to lay down one's life for one's friends.

We might lose The United Methodist Church. The church as we know it, with our enemies and our fears, will die. Facing death will not be easy. It is painful and terrifying. We are exposing our idols of financial security and denominational unity. We risk turning saints into enemies. We are offering up even our beloved connection. But when we love our church more than we love Christ, the body of Christ is already broken. When we preserve an institution instead of boldly loving whom Jesus loves, as Jesus loves, we will lose the very thing we tried to save.

Perhaps, after Jesus' way forward, all that will remain for the people called United Methodist will be the fullness of love. For following Jesus means doing as he did: emptying ourselves of all but love. It is this love that will lead us through the cross to new life as yet unknown. Do we expect to be made perfect in love in this life? By the grace of God, may the answer be "Yes!"

8

In Christ There Is No East or West

Eduard Khegay

Eduard Khegay is bishop of the Moscow Episcopal Area of The United Methodist Church.

NIKOLAI BERDYAEV, RUSSIAN RELIGIOUS philosopher, wrote in the beginning of the twentieth century that Russian thinking cannot be Eastern or Western.[1] He argued that both of these extremes are not appropriate. His hope for Russia was that she would grow to global leadership, and wake up the inner creative activity of the people. This reminds me of our global United Methodist Church and the importance of a multidimensional view when we deal with issues of our time. We as a church also cannot be Eastern or Western. We need to learn how to bless and enrich one another with our gifts and graces.

The purpose of my essay is to challenge our global church to look deeper. While the issue of human sexuality has moved to the top of our attention, I see it only as a trigger of deeper issues we face today.

In this essay, I will analyze our global movement from my Russian/Eurasian perspective. I will present my position on leadership, take a critical view of Western democracies, reflect on Scripture and Wesleyan tradition, and share my thoughts on unity.

I share this text in the spirit of humility and hope that you will not perceive it as a judgmental "expert's view," but accept it as a good challenge to look at our global church differently.

Crisis of Leadership

I love stories. They communicate values and have the power to transform lives. One story I learned from an American friend is about U.S. President Harry S Truman, who had a sign on his desk with the phrase "The buck stops here." He wanted to remember that as president he carried the ultimate responsibility for making decisions. This story reminds me of my role to lead and carry ultimate responsibility for my decisions as a bishop of The United Methodist Church. While I am convinced that each bishop works hard to lead his or her episcopal area, I find it very puzzling how we lead as the bishops collectively.

I realized at the 2016 General Conference that we have a crisis of leadership. It was quite surprising to hear from delegates that they wanted us, bishops, to lead. As bishops, didn't we already know that we needed to lead? It is obvious that our global church requires new ways of leading that are different from leading at local or even national levels. And while The UMC structure and decision-making processes can be improved and reinvented, what lies underneath is the way we as bishops relate to one another.

Can you imagine a fruitful organization that is led by leaders who do not fully trust one another and cannot have honest conversations? Can this team of leaders lead through intensified parliamentary procedures and learning more about legal issues? I cannot see how we can lead our global church this way. My prayers and hopes are that someday we as bishops will take more action to build trust and have honest conversations about challenges our church faces today.

For me, the litmus test of trust and honesty among leaders in the organization, especially the church, is how much is discussed in the official meetings and how much is discussed in the corridors. Can leaders trust one another enough to bring the same questions to the official meeting that they discuss in the corridors? Or do we simply want to be polite and politically correct so we do not offend one another? Since when have politeness and political correctness in the church become higher values than trust and honesty?

This brings us to the next important issue for our global UMC body: unity. The Methodist movement has enjoyed unity and faced divisions during several centuries of its history. We struggled with the issue of slavery. The Church of the Nazarene, for example, left The Methodist Church and challenged us to practice deeper holiness and simplicity. Our present debate on human sexuality has challenged our unity as a global church. Suddenly we have realized that we understand human sexuality and sexual orientation differently depending on geographic region, culture, theological background, and biblical interpretation. The more important question for me is this: can we have unity in The UMC without unity at the Council of Bishops? Again, unity at the council is related to the previously stated issue of trust and honesty.

Hey—maybe if I had ten million dollars today, I would invest them in building unity at the Council of Bishops! We need to figure out how to relate to one another and build a spirit of trust among ourselves. Can we model that for our global body? Some may find it too idealistic, given the fact that we speak several different languages, belong to multiple cultures, come from different continents, and live in extremely diverse economic and political systems. May we be reminded that the miracle of the Holy Spirit at Pentecost gave birth to our Christian church and united so many different people as they built trust and honesty in ministry with one another and to the world! The buck stops at the leadership level, and we as bishops have to figure this out. The present crisis of leadership can become an opportunity to do something we've never done before with transformational change and reform, leaving a long-lasting legacy for the future of The UMC.

Western Democracies and the Rest of Us

I have experienced several disillusionments in my life. One of them was during my life in the Soviet Union, when I realized that the Communism we were building was not actually the one that I read about in Lenin's books. I learned later that you cannot force people of the world to love Communism by using tanks and soldiers. Another disillusionment was when I studied in the United States. I realized that while democracy gives so many great opportunities and freedom to people, the people struggle with as much loneliness, racism, and addictions as they do in nondemocratic countries. I learned that you cannot force people of the world to love democracy by using airplanes and missiles. Here I want to juxtapose a few aspects of life to show that things are perceived and managed differently around the globe. And as a global denomination, we must take a serious look at these differences.

First, let's look at legal and relational differences. It is no secret to any United Methodist who has experienced another culture that, generally speaking, life in Western democracies is fast paced. People are goal oriented and busy. In most other places of the world, though, relationships are of such high value that being together is often more important than personal goals. As one who grew up in Kazakhstan, in the former Soviet Union, I love my Central Asian culture. And even after twenty plus years of living in Moscow, I feel much more comfortable in my hometown of Almaty, drinking tea with my friends and sharing our lives, than achieving another new result in the twenty-million–population megapolis of Moscow. That is not to say that we will not reach our goals. But as a global denomination, relationship must be our priority. Fifteen-minute coffee breaks will not do it—especially when coffee is not even my favorite drink!

The danger Western democracy projects onto the church is legalism. The way many of our Eurasian delegates experience General Conference is often very shocking. Legal matters, parliamentary procedures, appeals to Judicial Council, manipulations of points of order, disrespect toward presiding bishops—these are some of the things I have never experienced in my non-Western culture; and hope I never will. This is not the church I believe God desires to build. We read in the Acts of the Apostles: "Every day, they met together in the temple and ate in their homes. They shared food with gladness and simplicity. They praised God and demonstrated God's goodness to everyone. The Lord added daily to the community those who were being saved" (Acts of the Apostles 2:46-47, CEB). One can sense the spirit of relationship rather than legalism.

So maybe if I had ten million dollars today, I would invest them in building relationships among our people on a global level! Maybe that sounds too idealistic. Well, when I visit churches throughout my episcopal area, sometimes my Moscow goal-oriented drive is unsettled when we drink tea for three hours, or eat borsch soup for four hours, or when people ask me to visit their home briefly and we share our stories long after midnight. In the process I find myself puzzled as to when I start my "work." But after three days like that, I realize that people feel blessed and inspired by being able to share their stories with me, by being able to serve food for me and just be together, building relationships and friendships. Then I realize that building relationships is a higher goal than the one I had in mind. People are energized to grow in Christ and serve others through relationship. This is the beauty of relationships, and we need to develop this more on a global scale. Again, I would say that quick coffee breaks or even lunches (especially business lunches) won't do it.

Second, let's talk about human rights and morality. During the twentieth century, the Western democracies excelled at protecting human rights. Indeed, if not for Western democracies that promoted the value of human life and freedom of conscience, our world would likely have drifted more deeply into darkness. However, this focus has gone to the extreme during last few decades. To my cultural shock, I see teenagers manipulating the juvenile justice system; young people behaving disrespectfully toward elderly people in the name of freedom; and many propagating gay relationships as a norm and silencing those who stand for traditional families. I cannot accept that.

What I observe in Western democracies is that morality is often replaced with human rights. When I visited the Annual Conference of the Methodist Church in Britain some years ago, I heard one speaker from Samoa. He passionately challenged the audience with something like this: "When you came to us as missionaries you told us: 'Dress up!' [implying that Pacific Islanders' dress was improper for Christians to wear]. Now I come to you, fellow Methodists in Britain, and say: 'Dress up!' [implying the devaluation of morality in this Western democracy]."

I must share with you that I value and love many achievements of the Western democracies. I am forever grateful that I became a Christian because of a U.S. missionary. I feel so blessed to have studied in a U.S. seminary. Many people I admire in the Christian world come from Western Europe and the U.S.A. But in today's crisis of The United Methodist Church, I feel like part of our church in Western democratic countries acts like NATO, which keeps pushing its agenda and ignoring the United Nations. We do not want to repeat the same mistake NATO made in Iraq and Afghanistan. Our churches in the Western democratic countries cannot push their agenda on our global church, ignoring the fact that we are a worldwide body.

I hope our church continues to stand for human rights and teach people the value and sacredness of human life. But I hope even more that our church stands for morality and teaches people what God desires from us and what the Lord condemns. The extreme quest for human rights leads toward extreme individualism, which ignores the collectivism, solidarity, and shared morality so central to Christian experience and tradition. This is interconnected with the previous point on the relational aspect of Christian community and also brings us to the next point.

Third, worldly influence and holiness are critical to our future together as the church. One of the Ten Commandments tells us to observe the sabbath day and treat it as holy. God's example and God's design for creation teaches us holiness. As Christians, we are called holy in the Bible, people who are "called out" in this world—people who live by higher standards. We are people who are shaped by relationships with the Holy One every day. That changes everything.

What I observe in the countries with Western democracies is that worldly influence has gradually taken over some churches. Being moral and preaching holiness is not trendy anymore. Instead, individualistic desires to use marijuana freely, legalize weapons, redefine God-given understanding of family, and accumulate more wealth than one can use during a lifetime become modern idols. Many people living in other countries see this as the worldly attack on churches and Christian faith.

One may argue that we lose people because we are not trendy in the society. I would argue that we lose people because we do not consistently strive toward holiness. When you live a holy life, different from the world, you might risk people laughing at you or blaming you for not being loving or just. But Jesus walked this way before us, and he made it clear for people to understand what is holy and what is not. He spent time with the poor and outcasts of society, and he rebuked Pharisees and scribes. Jesus never played with the trendy influences of his time. His message was clear, challenging, unsettling, and transforming. He wants us to be holy because God is holy.

Why do I find these things of high importance for the United Methodist global body today? It is because we are a global body. But the problem is that we are managed as an organization within the Western democracy. And that brings me to my final point in this section.

Fourth, we must address the global nature of our church with its power, money, and politics. The history and nature of the Christian church is such that its leaders from Western democracies sent missionaries to spread the gospel into many continents. They had money and power. In many ways, the rest of us feel like children of our mother church. Our mother was proud of fast growth, exciting results, amazing Christian education, and the alleviation of poverty. She has gladly shared resources with her children. But children began to disagree with mother as her opinions on the issue of human sexuality changed. That is when children had to learn that, unfortunately, even in the church, power, money, and politics are very real.

Suddenly, the children learned that mother would no longer love and support them if they continued to disagree with her. It turned out that mother was no longer satisfied with how much her children contributed, although she had been happy to give them everything abundantly when they listened to her and followed her directions. She began to ignore her own democratic rules that she had taught her children to follow. The majority voice will not stop her because she has the power, money, and politics. She has become so political that her children can neither understand her nor even speak her language. She wants to keep pushing her agenda even if that means losing her children.

Scripture and Wesleyan Tradition

Conflicts and disagreements happened in the church historically, and they will continue to challenge our global church as we continue to learn what Scripture means for us today and how we continue to spread scriptural holiness throughout the land and strengthen our Wesleyan tradition. I am convinced that just as God created in the early church, God will create something new through this present conflict in the United Methodist movement. For some, it is a new interpretation of Scripture and a new definition of marriage. For others, it is renewed and strengthened traditional understanding of Scripture and marriage. It is obvious that these realities differ depending on the culture and context in which you live today. How do we continue as a global body? Let me give you one extreme illustration.

As you may know, polygamy is a reality in Africa. Our sisters and brothers have struggled with this issue for many years. Yet we as Christians hold the very orthodox position that monogamy is a norm. Can you imagine our sisters and brothers in Africa disturbing our General Conference with their protests, ignoring the voices around the world, and forcing us to bless polygamous marriages in our own contexts? I cannot imagine that.

Our Wesleyan tradition uses Scripture, reason, tradition, and experience as four authoritative sources together. The current crisis in our church challenges us to "test the spirits to see if they are from God" (1 John 4:1 CEB). One can see and feel how Scripture is picked and used to "baptize" what people want to believe rather than what the text says to us. Some people base their position heavily on the experience of their lives or the lives of their family members and friends. Others emphasize tradition that has kept the Christian church alive through the centuries and trials and persecution. The genius of the Wesleyan tradition is that we keep these four quadrilateral parts in creative tension and let the Spirit move us forward. Come, Holy Spirit, come!

What Is Unity?

The Book of Discipline of The United Methodist Church has been an important document, reflecting our unity among many things. Not anymore. Today in the year 2017, I cannot explain to my sisters and brothers in the Eurasia Episcopal Area why some United Methodists break the *Discipline* while others have to follow it. This is an important time for us to reflect again on what unity is.

As I envision the future of The United Methodist Church, I am confident that our church must have the unity of its leaders first. We need deep listening for one another and to learn from one another. We need to build trust and practice honesty. Where the covenant has been broken, we need time for restoration, healing, and a new level of relationship.

The buck stops with us bishops. I do hope and trust that the General Conference will make a new way forward for our global movement. This, however, would not automatically improve unity in the Council of Bishops and guarantee trust and honesty in our relationships. We need to do it—the sooner, the better.

Shared Christian values, morality, and holiness are important aspects of unity. You cannot have unity between husband and wife if one thinks that adulterous relationships are acceptable, while the other remains fully committed. I hope that our worldwide Methodist movement will constantly strive toward holiness and have a powerful witness with influence in the modern world—our modern world ruled by the "selfie-centered" lives of "my rights" and "my freedom." The Christian movement has always inspired people to be holy and be together rather than live "selfie" lives.

Our Christian faith is full of tension when it comes to power, money, and politics. How do we use these gifts and graces to sacrifice and empty ourselves, to deny ourselves, to take up our cross and follow the Holy One? Will we hold these gifts as weapons to fight, or will we be willing to be crucified with Christ and experience the Resurrection?

Let me conclude with my personal story. As I was writing this essay, presidents Donald Trump and Vladimir Putin had their first face-to-face meeting in Germany during the 2017 G20 Summit. I am perfectly aware that these two names awake a lot of emotions in us, both positive and negative. As a child of the Cold War who was told that Western countries were going to drop a nuclear bomb on the Soviet Union, I still remember those high school drills when we put gas masks on our faces and hid under the table to practice our actions in case of nuclear war. But God brought me to faith in Christ, and through our church I learned that I have sisters and brothers in Western countries who not only do not want war with us in the East, but they also love us as God loves them. They pray that God would use their presidents as instruments of peace. This was a transformational experience for me.

So, when I see presidents Trump and Putin talk with each other, I am hopeful and reminded of Nikolai Berdyaev's thought that we cannot be Eastern or Western. We are called to be together and bless one another whether we come from East or West, North or South. Like our church at Pentecost, let us continue to meet and share food with gladness and simplicity, listen to one another, praise our God, and serve others. And the Spirit of God will move us forward.

NOTES

1. Nikolai Berdyaev, *Sud'ba Rossii - Fate of Russia* (Moscow: Act, 2004), 42–43.

9

Unity with Division: John Wesley on the Church[1]

Scott T. Kisker

Scott T. Kisker is Professor of Church History and Associate Dean of Masters Programs at United Theological Seminary, Dayton, Ohio.

Introduction

> "[Schism] is evil in itself. To separate ourselves from a body of living Christians, with whom we were before united, is a grievous breach of the law of love. . . . It is only when our love grows cold, that we can think of separating from our brethren. . . . The pretenses for separation may be innumerable, but want of love is always the real cause; otherwise they would still hold the unity of the Spirit in the [bond] of peace. . . . And as such a separation is evil in itself, being a breach of brotherly love, so it brings forth evil fruit; it is naturally productive of the most mischievous consequences. It opens a door to all unkind tempers, both in ourselves and others. It leads directly to a whole train of evil surmising, to severe and uncharitable judging of each other. It gives occasion to offense, to anger and resentment, perhaps in ourselves as well as in our brethren; which, if not presently stopped, may issue in bitterness, malice, and settled hatred; creating a present hell wherever they are found, as a prelude to hell eternal."[2]

So wrote John Wesley on the nature of division or heresy (which he defined as the fomenting of division within communities of living Christians[3]).

With such a direct and strong statement against division, it is perhaps surprising that the Wesleyan Methodist tradition has produced as many bodies of Christians as it has, some living still: United Methodist, African Methodist Episcopal, African Methodist Episcopal Zion, Wesleyan Methodist, Free Methodist, Christian Methodist Episcopal, and Nazarene, to name a few, and these only within the confines of the United States. With a global perspective, given the independence of the descendants of British Methodism and the influence of Holiness and Pentecostalism, the divisions are legion. More surprising, given Wesley's words, than the "schisms" that flowed from our movement is the fact that our movement itself depends on schism, separation, division, for its very existence.

Wesleyan Methodism and Schism

Wesleyan Methodism was birthed in and through division.[4] In the mid-1730s, "Methodism" was a loose confederation of like-minded proponents of experiential Christianity and included what would later become Wesleyan Methodist under Wesley, Calvinistic Methodists under Whitefield, and the Moravian Church in England.

The divisions that led to these separate connections were not amicable. They involved passionate feelings on each side and real separation. These early "Methodists" divided over differences in theology, diverse readings of Scripture, community discipline, and liturgical practice. What we know as the Wesleyan tradition, with its emphasis on universal free grace, on human agency in salvation, on the means of grace, on the sacrament as a converting ordinance, on discipline, holiness, and perfection in love, is a product of these splits. To take an even broader view, were it not for church divisions (Imperial/Donatist, East/West, Protestant/Roman, Arminian/Reformed, Moravian/Anglo-Evangelical), Methodism would not exist as a coherent community to wrestle with identity.[5]

The Church?

That leaves the question hanging. Where is the church in all this? What is "the church" according to Wesleyan categories? Did these numerous divisions divide the "one, holy, catholic, and apostolic church" or (since Wesley found the Nicene Creed too politically compromised) the "holy catholic church"?[6] Were all earlier separations heretical? And which? Was Wesley a schismatic?

There is a clue to Wesley's ecclesiology in the sermon "On Schism," in which he opposes division. It shows that Wesley was not unaware of his own participation in the disputes that formed his connection. "If I could not continue united to any smaller society, church, or body of Christians," he wrote,

> without committing sin, without lying and hypocrisy, without preaching to others doctrines which I did not myself believe, I should be under an absolute necessity of separating from that society. And in all these cases the sin of separation, with all the evils consequent upon it, would not lie upon it, would not lie upon me, but upon those who constrained me to make that separation, by requiring of me such terms of communion as I could not in conscience comply with.[7]

Wesley even admitted that (if forbidden to do what God had called him to do in preaching the gospel) he would separate from the Church of England[8] (a church he thought was the best visible instantiation of primitive Christianity, and with whom he mostly agreed on matters of doctrine, discipline, polity, and liturgy) if its discipline threatened to stop the mission of Methodism to which he was called.

Another clue is that Wesley never assumed that those who disagreed with him—from whom he had separated institutionally, missionally, and who were even in a separate communion—were not true Christians, not members of the holy catholic church.

A Wesleyan Ecclesiology

The Oneness of the Church

If unity, given the founding logic of the Wesleyan movement, does not primarily exist institutionally or even ritually in a shared sacrament of the

Eucharist, where does it exist? In his 1785 sermon "Of the Church," Wesley reflected on this question using Ephesians 4:1-6, where he interpreted each of Paul's statements of unity: one body, one Spirit, one calling, one Lord, one faith, one baptism, one God and Father of all, to turn aside any understanding of the unity of the universal church as primarily institutionally visible, or necessitating connection to one organization.

Members of the universal church share in the one Spirit "who animates all . . . the *living* members of the Church of God."[9] They share "a hope full of immortality. They know, to die is not to be lost: Their prospect extends beyond the grave."[10] They have one Lord who "reigns over all those that are partakers of this hope. To obey him, to run the way of his commandments, is their glory and joy."[11] They have one faith, "the free gift of God . . . teaching them to say with holy boldness 'My Lord and My God.'"[12] They share "one baptism; which is the outward sign our one Lord has been pleased to appoint, of all that inward and spiritual grace which he is continually bestowing upon his Church."[13] Finally, "There is 'one God and Father of all' who have the Spirit of adoption, which 'crieth in their hearts, Abba, Father;' which 'witnesseth' continually 'with their spirits,' that they are the children of God."[14] And "the catholic or universal Church is, all the persons in the universe whom God hath so called out of the world as to entitle them to the preceding character."[15]

This definition of the one church, Wesley argued, *can* be read as consistent with the Anglican Article of Religion 19: "The visible Church of Christ is a congregation of faithful men."

However, while not opposed to the doctrinal standard of his own communion, Wesley clearly thought the article, where it reads "in which the pure word of God is preached, and the sacraments be duly administered,"[16] overreached. "The Article" Wesley says, "includes a little more than the Apostle has expressed,"[17] and he would "not undertake to defend" *that* statement.[18] His objection was precisely because he believed membership in Christ's church to be about whether one is being saved. It is not opinions over teachings or modes of worship.[19]

The "oneness" of the church is a unity through shared experience of the new birth and changed character, not encompassed in any particular organization or even through the sacramental sign of its true communion. In "Predestination Calmly Considered" (which is not very calm and hardly a text promoting external unity), Wesley referred to the true church as "those who are grafted into the good olive tree . . . not barely the outward, visible church but the invisible, consisting of holy believers."[20] Unity is through our invisible participation in Christ.

Plurality in Unity

According to Wesley, the universal church will not be one of outward connection. First, because the outward visible church includes non-Christians, people who are not part of the unity of the body of Christ. In the outward visible church "reprobates are . . . mingled with the elect," as St. Augustine put it.[21] There are "weeds and wheat," to quote another learned theologian.[22] "How clear is this! If the Church, as to the very essence of it, is a body of believers," wrote Wesley.[23]

Second, each "outward visible church" is constituted by people who share "opinions"—on doctrine, discipline, and modes of worship. Such shared opinions are necessary, constituent aspects of community cohesion, and yet they separate even true Christians from one another. "A catholic spirit is not indifference to all congregations," or even connections. That is "absurd and unscriptural."[24]

There will always be multiple separate groups containing real Christians, because "every wise man will allow others the same liberty of thinking which he desires [others] should allow him."[25] Unity does "not mean," according to Wesley, "'be of my opinion.' You need not."[26] That cannot be desired or expected, even though differing opinions with regard to Christian teaching divide Christians. Of course, true believers across separate connections bear "with those who differ."[27] A believer "only asks [another believer in a different connection] . . . to unite in that single question, 'Is thy heart right, as my heart is with thy heart.'"[28] But because of differences of opinion, the church will be an institutionally divided union in faith, even among true believers, until Christ returns.

A Witness to the Presence of the One Church

While such differences "in opinions or modes of worship may prevent an entire external union,"[29] there are always signs of the presence of the invisible church. Despite outward division, there must be a physical gathering, a connection. There is no holiness that is not "social holiness," that does not involve social commitments to other human beings. Believers unite. Such a gathering, according to Wesley, may be "any number of people, how small or great soever"[30] It may be as small as two or three, who share "one body" and "one calling . . . out of the world, (so the original word properly signifies,) uniting together in one congregation."[31]

However, the most important visible evidence of the true church is holiness. "The Church" (and here Wesley meant the invisible unity of believers) "is called holy, because it is holy, because every member thereof is holy, though in different degrees, as He that called them is holy."[32] This "olive tree," wrote Wesley, "is the invisible Church, for it 'consists of holy believers' which none but the invisible Church does."[33]

The Roots of Wesleyan Ecclesiology

This invisible understanding of "catholic unity" had been carried down through the centuries by a number of religious communities. Most proximately to Wesley, this ecclesiology was developed and passed on through Pietism. Wesley's ideas about "church," while certainly influenced by his eighteenth-century Anglican context (mostly in aspects he referred to as "opinions"), were much more influenced by this less institutionally defined movement.

Pietists expected Christians to behave differently in this world because they had encountered another world. Believers were expected to have a quasi-mystical experience of faith that would result in holy living. Christians were not simply declared righteous but actually made righteous by the power of the Holy Spirit. Furthermore, the Spirit's work in individuals meant one could expect the Spirit's work in the world, through mercy, mission, and social reform.[34]

Pietism had theological emphases yet was not doctrinal in the way magisterial churches understood it. It distinguished between theological "fundamentals" and "opinions"[35] and thus moved and multiplied across confessional borders. Wrong opinions (within a certain range, anyway) did not make transforming faith impossible. Pietism had institutional form, namely, the use of small groups for cultivating piety, but its unity was not defined institutionally. Pietists did not limit fellowship or missional cooperation across confessional lines.[36] Rather, true unity in Christ was demonstrated in shared fellowship and missional cooperation across ecclesial divisions. Their ecclesiology acknowledged common cause and care across divisions of doctrine, and practice, yet did not seek to eradicate the divisions.

Visually, we might conceive of this ecclesiology as a sort of daisy[37] with each petal being a congregation, connection, or denomination in which Christians gather. Each petal shares peculiar opinions, modes of worship, and practices of leadership and discipline that distinguish it from other "petals." The center circle, intersecting all petals, is the true church. There are faithful people in each petal. But not every participant in a given set of opinions, modes of worship, and discipline is within the true church. Not all have saving faith. The true church is a circumscribed "body" of some within each "petal," who are vitally connected to Christ by faith.

The true church is visible within each various institutional church (and is what enables them to be called "churches"). It is visible to the outside world through holiness, through its departure from the patterns of the world and submission to the patterns of Christ's reign. Unity of the church, however, exists at the center, in Christ. It is unity of fellowship, missional cooperation, and mutual recognition across division. Therefore, a division within a

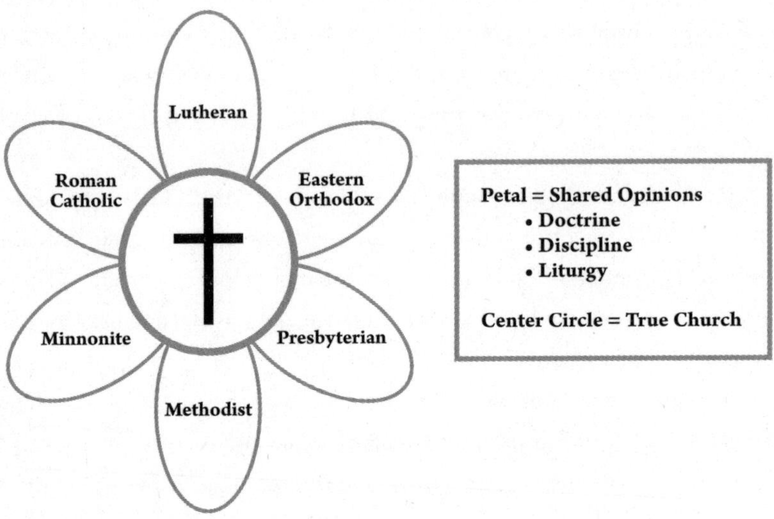

particular petal cannot touch this unity, has no effect on the unity of the true church, cannot touch those who remain "engrafted into the good olive tree."[38]

Conclusions

So what do we make of this heritage, this ecclesiology, and its instantiation within the Wesleyan movement from its inception? Let me draw a few observations that may help us in our present predicament as a denomination:

1. United Methodism should embrace the reality that its ecclesiology is defined primarily not through Imperial and Magisterial categories but through more radical (with assumptions about holiness and discipline) categories by way of Pietism. The very existence of The United Methodist Church, with its reformation roots in Anglican (The Methodist Church), Lutheran (The Evangelical Alliance), Reformed, and Anabaptist (the United Brethren in Christ) traditions, makes this obvious. The union of Mennonite and Reformed traditions in the

United Brethren is another clear instance. Only this Pietistic ecclesiology makes sense of Wesley's writings on schism and the church and the reality of Wesleyan Methodism's origins.

2. United Methodism should abandon any argument that the integrity of a fifty-year-old denomination of Protestants impacts the unity of the church. Any pretense of institutional unity ended with the Donatist controversy in the fourth century, if not before that. Furthermore, external institutional unity cannot be held as paramount over other Nicene creedal marks of the church, especially those shared with the Apostles' Creed (which Wesley greatly preferred): sanctity and catholicity.
3. Methodism, in line with its ecclesiological heritage, should embrace a robust defense of denominationalism. The church is the communion of saints. It includes those in all congregations, connections, traditions, and denominations who have true saving faith. Institutional expressions of church (which necessitate actually and firmly held "opinions" on doctrine, discipline, polity, and liturgy) are churches insofar as they contain said saints gathered to worship, serve God, and hold one another accountable. Where believers meet, they participate in the true church. But no gathering or connection encapsulates the catholic body of Christ, nor is the body of Christ fully encapsulated in any gathering or connection. Correct opinions do not ensure participation in the "true church."
4. United Methodism should, by the logic of our history and ecclesiology, acknowledge that there are legitimate reasons to go separate ways in separate connections. Without separations, we would not have a Methodist tradition worth preserving or dividing over. Furthermore, if we cannot hold one another accountable to any coherent expression of Christian ethics, if we cannot agree on explications of the General Rules, we are no longer one church, in the Wesleyan sense. The practices that constitute our legitimate ecclesial order (the General Rules,

oversight, classes, bands, conferencing, and itinerancy) have already been abrogated. We can no longer "walk together."

5. Finally, United Methodism should realize that should a split occur, by the logic of our ecclesiology, there will be no "pure church" on the other side of it. No schism produces a church that is *the* church, prior to the eschaton. There are always faithless people within any body called "church," sharing the "opinions" necessary to hold together corporately. There are also always people, genuinely grafted in to the true vine, which is Christ, who do not agree with the opinions of my congregation, my connection, my denomination. One can be wrong and be "being saved."[39] Thank God.

NOTES

1. Originally appeared under the title "Applying What Wesley Taught About Schism," in *Circuit Rider*, vol. 41, no. 4, August/September/October 2017.
2. John Wesley, Sermon 75, "On Schism," [II]:11-12, in *Sermons III*, ed. Albert C. Outler, vol. 3 of *The Bicentennial Edition of the Works of John Wesley* (Nashville: Abingdon Press, 1976), 64–65. Note that the damage in schism is not to a structure, but to the character of holiness in those who participate in it.
3. Wesley, "On Schism," I:6, *Works*, 3:62.
4. Some will assume this refers to the beginnings of the Methodist Episcopal Church in 1784, when a Methodist church became officially and organizationally independent from anything known as the Anglican Church. It does not. This was not a schism but a development necessitated by abandonment. The Anglican Church had ceased to exist in America—*de facto* when Anglican clergy fled to Canada or England in the 1770s, and *de jure* by the former colonies' independence from the Supreme Governor of the Church, the King. In 1784 there was technically no Anglican Church in the United States from which Methodists could split. The Protestant Episcopal Church was not formed until 1789. Ironically, one of Wesley's former Methodist lay missionaries to America, Joseph Pilmore, became one of its early priests. The schisms

that formed Wesleyan Methodism as a distinct tradition had happened fifty years earlier.

5. In many aspects, Methodism preserves a strain of holiness and charismatic ecclesiology, which is not easily traced through the standard line of institutional "orthodoxy."
6. Wesley preferred the Apostles' Creed. See Wesley, Sermon 74, "Of the Church," [III]:28, *Works,* 3:55. He also intentionally removed the Nicene Creed from the Articles of Religion and liturgy that he sent to America. Compare Article VIII "Of the Creed" of the Articles of the Church of England, which is omitted from the Articles of Religion sent by Wesley to America. See also John Wesley, *Sunday Service of the Methodists, with other Occasional Services.*
7. Wesley, Sermon 75, "On Schism," [II]:17, *Works,* 3:67.
8. Ibid., [II]:17, 67.
9. Ibid., [I]:8, 48–49.
10. Ibid., [I]:9, 49.
11. Ibid., [I]:10, 49.
12. Ibid., [I]:11, 49.
13. Ibid., [I]:12, 49.
14. Ibid., [I]:13, 50.
15. Ibid., [I]:14, 50.
16. Ibid., [I]:16, 51.
17. Ibid.
18. Wesley, "Of the Church," [I]:19, *Works,* 3:52.
19. Ibid., [I]:19, 52.
20. John Wesley, "Predestination Calmly Considered," in *John Wesley,* ed. Albert C. Outler (New York: Oxford University Press, 1964), 461.
21. Augustine of Hippo, *City of God,* 18.49.
22. Matthew 13:24-30.
23. Wesley, "Of the Church," [III]:28, *Works,* 3:56.
24. Ibid., III:3, 93.
25. Ibid., I:6, 84.
26. Ibid., II:1, 89.
27. Ibid., I:6, 84.
28. Ibid., I:6, 84–85.
29. Ibid., Intro:4, 82.
30. Wesley, "Of the Church," Intro:2, *Works,* 3:46.

31. Ibid., Intro:3, 47.
32. Wesley, "Of the Church," [III]:28, *Works*, 3:55–56.
33. Wesley, "Predestination Calmly Considered," 461.
34. Dale Brown, *Understanding Pietism* (Grand Rapids: Eerdmans, 1978), 27–28.
35. This distinction is the origin of the contemporary language of "fundamentalism." The nineteenth-century publishers of "The Fundamentals" were arguing that the supernatural essence of Christianity was threatened by liberalism, and that was not a matter of "opinion" but "fundamental" to the gospel.
36. The first corresponding member of the Society for Propagating Christian Knowledge, an organization with roots in the Anglican Pietist movement known as the Religious Societies Movement, was the leader of the German Pietist Halle Foundation, August Herman Francke. In his letter of introduction to the society, he wrote, "I look upon these things as comfortable signs that the Spirit of God is now about a great work to put a new face on the whole Christian Church."
37. The Reformed have their T.U.L.I.P. Why shouldn't we Wesleyans have a flower too?
38. Wesley, "Predestination Calmly Considered," 461.
39. Acts 2:47; 27:20; 1 Corinthians 1:18; 15:2; 2 Corinthians 2:15.

10

A Gracious Way Forward

Thomas A. Lambrecht

Thomas A. Lambrecht is vice president of Good News and a member of the Bishops' Commission on a Way Forward.

FOR MORE THAN TWO THOUSAND years there has been a unified global vision for Christian marriage and human sexuality. In every culture, on every continent, and in every language around the globe, Christianity's teaching has always promoted the exclusive belief that one man and one woman in lifelong marriage optimizes human flourishing within society. It is a foundational belief shared in common within Catholicism, Orthodoxy, and Protestantism. United Methodism has always taught that the anchor for intimate relationships for clergy and laity should be fidelity in marriage and celibacy in singleness.

After two millennia, a contrary teaching has been introduced within segments of North American and European mainline denominations. It proposes that contemporary same-sex marriage and intimacy is not the same thing as that prohibited by certain biblical passages. It proposes that mutual, loving same-sex relationships can and should exist today—and should be blessed by the worldwide United Methodist Church. From the viewpoint of progressives, contemporary scientific understandings about the origins of sexual orientation make it likely that same-sex attraction is an inborn characteristic. Therefore, they believe same-sex relations can be holy and good if engaged in within the parameters of faithfulness and mutuality. Accordingly, they believe, the church ought to condone same-sex relationships, perform same-sex marriages, and ordain non-celibate lesbians and gays into ministry.

These two positions tend to be mutually exclusive. The differences between them are stark and irreconcilable. Underlying the two positions are often different views about biblical authority and inspiration, different definitions of holiness, and different understandings of what it means to be a disciple of Jesus Christ.

Thus, it is nearly impossible for many people holding the two different positions to share a common mission of making disciples for the transformation of the world. For one, transforming the world means working for the full equality, acceptance, and affirmation of LGBTQ persons and their relationships and their full inclusion in the church. For the other, transforming the world means promoting traditional views of marriage and sexuality. The two are working at cross purposes and in opposition to each other!

How are we as Christians to treat one another and live together in one church, given that each might see the other as embracing a wrong-headed theology? How can we keep the vitriol that characterizes the political discussions in the U.S. today from polluting our church and destroying the relationships we have as brothers and sisters in Christ?

Love One Another

Of course, the bottom line for Christians is that we are to love one another. This is the way our love for God is expressed in a horizontal dimension. It is one of the two greatest commandments (Matthew 22:32-40). But what does it really mean to love? Our society has so distorted the meaning of the word that we have a difficult time knowing what love really is.

One passage of Scripture that has been meaningful to me in helping guide my thinking and behavior has been verses from Philippians 2. "Your attitude should be the same as that of Christ Jesus" (v. 5 NIV 1984). "Do nothing out of selfish ambition or vain conceit, but in humility consider others better than yourselves. Each of you should look not only to your own interests, but also to the interests of others" (vv. 3-4 NIV 1984).

Our motivation in engaging with one another over this controversial and sensitive topic should not be "selfish ambition or vain conceit." We should not use this conflict to build our own power base or achieve worldly success. Instead, we ought to be prayerfully seeking the truth. Our concern ought not to be whether we are on the right side of man-made history, but on the right side of God's will. After all, being a disciple means submitting completely to Jesus Christ as Lord, subsuming our wills to his. We seek not our judgment, but his; not our understanding, but his.

Humility

This requires humility. As Paul reminds us, "we know in part" (1 Corinthians 13:9 NIV). Our knowledge is imperfect; our understanding is impaired by the sin and brokenness that permeates this world. We have to acknowledge we could be wrong. We believe (even strongly) we are right, but we might be mistaken. That brother or sister with whom we vehemently disagree might actually be right! I don't think so, but I have to be honest about the possibility.

That means I need to hold my position firmly, but lightly. I need to have a teachable spirit and a desire to continue learning and growing in my understanding of God, the Bible, and people. I have been studying this question for nearly thirty-five years, and I am still learning things I did not know.

Having humility also humanizes the people with whom I am in conflict. They are not abstract "enemies," but fellow human beings, made in God's image like me, hopefully even brothers and sisters in Christ who share a deep love for Jesus. When I recognize people in that way, I will talk to them and about them differently. Personal attacks and ridicule have no place in a humble, mutual search for truth.

My wife is a marriage and family therapist, and she is constantly telling her clients (and me) to give the other person the benefit of the doubt. Believe the best about people, rather than the worst. Put the best possible interpretation on what someone is saying, rather than the worst.

That approach is tough to take when trust is in short supply. Whether it is in a troubled marriage or in a church riven by conflict, it is easy to demonize the other person, ascribe bad motives, make unwarranted assumptions, and hear what people say in the worst possible light.

Taking a Higher Road

As Christians, we are called to a higher road. We can be an example to the world not because we agree on everything, but in how we disagree with one another. The second-century Christian leader Tertullian wrote that non-Christians would be drawn to Christ when they could say of Christians, "see how they love one another . . . and how they are ready to die for one another." Would you give your life for one of the people with whom you vehemently disagree?

We may not need to literally give our lives for another, but we are called to sacrifice self by looking to the interests of others, not only our own. In other words, I should seek what is best for you, with whom I disagree, and not just what is best for me. One definition of love is seeking what is best for another. (Of course, we need to refrain from thinking we know what is best for another person and accordingly imposing that upon them. Such a patronizing approach is not love, but power. God has given parents that responsibility toward their minor children, but it is not a universal right to treat other adults that way.)

Considering the interests of others is an important part of the work of the Bishops' Commission on a Way Forward for the church. As a diverse and representative group, we are called not just to advocate for the interests of our particular part of the church, but to seek the good of the whole church. To do that, we must consider how to satisfy the legitimate needs of other parts of the church with which we disagree. Only by doing so can we arrive at a solution that is comprehensive, fair, and God-honoring.

How The United Methodist Church resolves the intractable conflict in our church is just as important as the content of the resolution.

Understanding the Problem

One aspect of mutual respect is to attempt to understand the perspectives of those with whom we disagree. I write from the viewpoint of one who believes that the current position of our *Book of Discipline* reflects a balanced and biblically faithful perspective on ministry with LGBTQ persons. I have also had extensive conversations with persons who have different perspectives. Understanding these various perspectives is essential to finding a godly way to live with one another.

The document "In Search of Unity,"[1] published in 1998 as the report of a theological dialogue about the tensions in The United Methodist Church, presents an analysis first articulated by now-retired Bishop Judith Craig. The church is not only divided between those who have a traditional understanding of marriage as between one man and one woman, versus those who have a more progressive understanding of marriage as between any two persons, regardless of gender. The church is also divided between those who can live with a variety of opinions and practices of ministry around LGBTQ persons ("compatibilists"), versus those who believe that the church's position is of essential importance and cannot live in a church where the other viewpoint is promoted and practiced ("incompatibilists").

Progressive Incompatibilists

Progressive incompatibilists "believe that the exclusion of anyone from the full life of the church is completely unacceptable because it is contradictory to the gospel. For them, homosexual persons, practicing or not, are persons of sacred worth living according to the gifts and evidences of God's grace given to them. To deny such persons a full place in the church is a violation of the holiness and catholicity of the church. For these incompatibilists, to continue to participate in such an exclusive and oppressive organization only serves to legitimate the incomplete worshipping community and perpetuate the sin of exclusion. Commitment to the church of Jesus Christ requires active resistance and the commitment to stand prophetically against the injustices perpetuated by the institution."[2]

It is the progressive incompatibilist approach that has caused clergy (including one retired bishop) to perform same-sex weddings, contrary to our *Book of Discipline*, sometimes as a public protest event. This approach has prompted seven annual conferences and two jurisdictions to pass resolutions of non-conformity with the *Book of Discipline*. It has resulted in annual conference boards of ordained ministry recommending for ordination persons whom they knew to be practicing homosexuals. And it has led to the Western Jurisdiction electing and consecrating the Rev. Karen Oliveto, a married lesbian, as a United Methodist bishop.

The actions of progressive incompatibilists are an expression of their quest for justice and the rights of LGBTQ persons within the context of our church. They see this quest as informed and commanded by Scripture and the teachings of Jesus. They have come to the place where they cannot live in a denomination that does not marry or ordain gays and lesbians. So they have taken matters into their own hands and created a *de facto* reality in many annual conferences that is contrary to the position of The United Methodist Church.

Traditional Incompatibilists

Traditional incompatibilists, on the other hand, believe "for the United Methodist Church to accept homosexual practices either officially in its courts or unofficially by condoning widespread practice would be to forfeit its designation as a body of faithful people where the pure Word of God is preached and the sacraments duly administered according to Christ's ordinance. For these incompatibilists their stance is a matter of conscience as formed by scripture and the doctrinal standards of The United Methodist Church. Furthermore, most incompatibilists on the more conservative side believe that the classical teaching of the Christian tradition is a much-needed word of healing. It is a precious medicine that the Holy Spirit can use to transform and redeem all our sexual sins and wounds. Hence they cannot but proclaim and implement the full liberty from all sin promised in the gospel and warranted by the Lordship of Jesus Christ."[3] Traditional incompatibilists believe the church has unofficially changed its position by its inability to hold accountable those who have violated the teachings and requirements of the church. This has prompted a number of large congregations to leave The United Methodist Church and is causing thousands of individuals to leave their local congregations or withhold financial support for the church.

Compatibilists

Compatibilists, whether progressive or traditional, are willing to live in a church where they can practice ministry as they feel led, without being blocked or prohibited by the other perspective. Progressive compatibilists want to be able to marry and ordain gays and lesbians, but they are willing to live in a denomination where others do not. Traditional compatibilists are not willing to perform same-sex weddings or accept practicing gay or lesbian pastors in their churches, but they are willing to live in a denomination where others do.

Implications

Currently, many if not most progressive incompatibilists seem willing to live in a denomination that allows, but does not require, same-sex weddings and ordination of practicing LGBTQ persons. The shared support of progressive incompatibilists and compatibilists of every stripe has given rise to compatibilist approaches, from the Hamilton-Slaughter "agree to disagree" to the "local option" to the "Third Way" from the Connectional Table. All had in common the creation of a compatibilist denomination that allows different forms of beliefs and ministries to function within one organization.

This compatibilist approach, however, ignores the interests of traditional incompatibilists, who cannot live in a denomination where what they see as disobedience to the clear teaching of Scripture is allowed. U.S. traditional incompatibilists and those from the central conferences outside the U.S.—notably in Africa and much of the Philippines and Eastern Europe—constitute a majority of the church as reflected in the delegation at the 2016 General Conference.

Any attempt to engage in mutually respectful ways of living in the Wesleyan tradition amid the current crisis must reckon with the conflicting interests reflected in the incompatibilist groups. Progressive incompatibilists need to have a Wesleyan denomination that allows same-sex marriage and ordination of practicing homosexuals. They will keep fighting until they get one. The only way to stop the conflict is to give them their own denomination, whether it is by evicting them from the current United Methodist Church or by some form of negotiated separation.

Evicting progressives would take eight to twenty years and would involve an even more hard-nosed fight within the denomination than we have currently witnessed (and even that might not be successful). Is this truly how Christ would have us treat one another? And the fight to evict progressives would be all-consuming, meaning that the mission and ministry of The United Methodist Church would suffer, and our denominational decline in the U.S. would accelerate.

Traditional incompatibilists need to have a Wesleyan denomination that disallows same-sex marriage and ordination of practicing homosexuals in order to remain true to their understanding of Scripture. Traditionalists currently hold the majority at General Conference. So the only way for progressives to change the position of the church is to evict traditionalists or have some form of negotiated separation. Some progressive annual conferences have engaged in evicting traditionalists over the years by not accepting traditionalist candidates for ordination, marginalizing traditionalists from conference leadership, or giving undesirable appointments to traditionalist clergy. But again, is this how Christ would have us treat one another?

I believe the only way we can authentically bear witness to a graceful and respectful way of treating one another is to adopt the Isaiah model. "'Come now, and let us reason together,' says the Lord" (Isaiah 1:18 KJV). We need to reason with one another and arrive at a mutually acceptable solution that honors the needs and interests of all parties as much as possible. The choice between forcing people to live within a denomination with which they fundamentally disagree or forcing people to leave a denomination that they love is an unholy quandary. If, because of our theological commitments, we are unable to model a unified witness, may we not at least model a loving and respectful one?

NOTES

1. "In Search of Unity" Document, http://www.umaffirm.org/cornet/unity.html; 8. Accessed November 17, 2017.
2. Ibid.
3. Ibid.

11

We Can . . . We Must

Tracy S. Malone

Tracy S. Malone is resident bishop, Ohio East Episcopal Area, The United Methodist Church.

The Urgent Need

SOCIETIES EVERYWHERE IN THE WORLD are increasingly divided, hateful, and violent. Gun violence kills innocents. Abusive power restricts freedoms. Racial discord tears apart communities. Ungenerous acts and assertions marginalize LGBTQI persons. Too often in the United States, black and brown people cannot trust those who are supposed to serve and protect them. Opioid addiction is at an all-time high and is destroying lives.

Suicide is on the rise, especially among young people. Families are separated by unjust immigration policies. Our political climates make us anxious, fearful, and suspicious of one another because of divisive and mean-spirited rhetoric, policies, and behaviors.

We can do better. We must do better. We are the heirs of Susanna and John Wesley, Martin Luther King, Jr., James Thomas, Leontyne Kelley, and Jesse DeWitt. Like these saints, we too are preparers of the way for the advent of God's love and redemptive work in the world. As followers of Christ, and as a people called United Methodists, we are bearers of the good news of Jesus.

Our mission is to tear down the walls of hate, division, and fear. To disciple, build, and sustain authentic loving communities. To do justice and to restore hope where there is brokenness and pain.

As baptized believers, we promise to "renounce the spiritual forces of wickedness, reject the evil powers of this world, repent of our sin and accept the freedom and power God gives us to resist evil, injustice, and oppression in whatever forms they present themselves" (Baptismal Covenant I, *The United Methodist Hymnal*).[1] What has been asked of earlier generations is now required of us: If not us, then who? If not now, when?

Bound together by covenant and shared labors, we are The United Methodist Church, bearing witness to God's love, grace, justice, and unity. This is not easy work. It is not for the timid or the reluctant. Doing justice and loving mercy is a way of life. Formed and empowered by the Spirit as the people of faith, we are strengthened and prepared to bear witness to the world.

For forty-five years our church has been discerning and debating how we will express our love of God and neighbor amid intense disagreements about the nature of homosexuality, the ethics of sexual practices among same-gender persons, and the church's teachings about marriage and qualifications for ordination. Our disagreements seem as intractable as they are painful.

Persons of good will and deep faith have grappled with conflicting interpretations of Scripture; debated the relevance of various scientific findings; and have had their hearts broken by the pain and anxiety of sons, daughters, and others who have felt excluded and rejected. The strains of those disputes have worn the nerve endings and patience of people of all views. This has sometimes pitted neighbor against neighbor and has resulted in open conflict and deepening anguish among the people called United Methodists.

And so, just like the larger society, we too have become increasingly divided, and our rhetoric and our actions toward one another have become ever more confrontational. We too witness antagonistic acts and assertions, and the clamor of disputed claims of differing groups makes us anxious, fearful, and suspicious of one another. And our divisive and angry rhetoric and increasingly litigious ways of relating to one another drown out our testimonies of God's good news to a world hungry for salvation and hope.

Our Time Is Now

Enough with the battles and the complaints against one another! We can do better. We must. By grace we have been made anew, and our mission is to invite persons into a deep and transforming relationship with Jesus Christ. Let's turn our attention to being co-laborers—joining in God's work of love and redemption for all of creation.

In recognition of the burning need to show a better and more perfect way forward, the 2016 General Conference mandated that the Council of Bishops "lead The United Methodist Church in discerning and proposing a way forward through the present impasse related to human sexuality and to explore options that help to maintain and strengthen the unity of the church."[2] All of us must now ready ourselves for the fruits of that faithful work of listening and envisioning. Our task in turn is to receive the resulting recommendations and with new vigor turn our attention to God's work of making disciples of Jesus Christ for the transformation of our hurting world.

Called by God

We must not neglect our vocation, which is the ministry of all Christians. Paul speaks for himself and to us in 2 Timothy: "I was appointed a messenger, apostle, and teacher of this good news. . . . I know the one in whom I've placed my trust. I'm convinced that God is powerful enough to protect what he has placed in my trust " (2 Timothy 1:11-12 CEB).

Paul's public declaration reveals his courageous conviction about his assignment but also calls forth our own. This essential responsibility for being messengers and teachers of good news is deeply rooted in our experience of God as creator, sustainer, and redeemer.

So full and invigorating is this conviction that wells up from the center of Paul's being and from our own, that like him we are persuaded that nothing in life or death shall separate us from God's love and grace. Nothing present and nothing to come, no hardship, tribulation, distress, persecution, peril, or sword. And that gives us the courage to be peacemakers, advocates for mercy and for justice in the places we serve and live.

What an incredible surge of assurance this is! This is the faith that surpasses all understanding. As people called by God, lay and clergy, we celebrate the manifestation of the Spirit working through us. We remember and give thanks that in our faith journey we have said "Yes, here I am, send me," in response to God's claim on us, and we recommit ourselves to love and serve in the name of Jesus.

This is how we prepare and make ourselves ready for the work to come. We are equipped to live, proclaim, love, and serve with courageous conviction, confident that God's Spirit has anointed us for holy and sacred work. We are not undone by the heartbreak, anxiety, discord, and conflict that have marked previous discussions about how to live with our different understandings about human sexuality. On the contrary, we are propelled and encouraged for the journey ahead as we follow Jesus, who offers unconditional love by doing justice, loving mercy, and walking humbly with God.

Ready to Lead

Deep faith is expressed in prayerful convictions that animate courageous and bold leadership. Leaders are not mere spectators; they take responsibility and move forward to do all the good they can in all the ways they can for as long as they can.

When we are convicted by God's call and sustained by God's provision for our lives, we are empowered to lead with courage. We shout with assurance that nothing is impossible for God and that God's good grace is sufficient for the living of these days.

In 2 Timothy we discover three significant convictions in Paul's prayer that edify and embolden us.

Keep alive the gift

"I'm reminded of your authentic faith. . . . I'm sure that this faith is also inside you" (2 Timothy 1:5 CEB).

Paul tells Timothy that "I'm sure that this faith is also inside you" because he knows he will need to take it with him as he moves out to meet a world full of fear and conflict.

The ministry of the baptized calls us out of our comfort zone and into the mission field. Just beyond our familiar territory are the places at the margins where suffering, despair, poverty, and oppression are found. Those are places for us to invest our lives—being with the folks in the prisons, hospitals, and drug houses; caring and advocating for the children in our schools and the workers in fields and factories. We know how to stand with God's people wherever there is need for doing justice and loving mercy in both the private and public arenas. And we need to do this today, in this particular time, for our brothers and sisters who are crying out for justice and mercy from our own church.

As leaders, we are called into uncomfortable and unfamiliar places. We confront our fears; we ask hard questions and open our minds and hearts to the fresh winds of the Spirit that give us insight and compassion. We go to the places we had not dared to go, meet the people we have not dared to talk and walk with; we learn to show love in places where we find it difficult to show love; we work for justice where we've previously shown no mercy.

There is no escaping it. This is challenging, difficult, fearful work. We are bound to get discouraged, distracted, sometimes defeated; and we may become disillusioned. And that's precisely when we return to find encouragement in Paul's guidance to Timothy.

Eugene Petersen says it this way, "We had nothing to do with it. It was all *his* idea, a gift prepared for us in Jesus long before we knew anything about it" (2 Timothy 1:9 MSG). And as Paul writes, "Protect this good thing that has been placed in your trust through the Holy Spirit who lives in us" (2 Timothy 1:14 CEB).

Keep alive the gift that is in you.

Be bold in your witness

"God didn't give us a spirit that is timid but one that is powerful, loving, and self-controlled" (2 Timothy 1:7 CEB).

Confronted by disputes, anger, and difficult issues, we might hesitate to be bold and prophetic in our witness. But God has not given us a spirit of fear. God has given us power, love, and self-control. We in turn must teach and model how God's love and grace transcends hatred, fear, and division. Our experience of grace in our lives compels us to defy the world's boundaries of who's in and who's out, who is welcome and who is not. We must not be apologetic but unflinching as we joyfully proclaim God's good news for all.

We must be bold:

- Relying on the power of God that is at work in us
- Serving as a voice for the voiceless
- Speaking truth in love to power
- Doing what is right instead of what is popular or expected
- Teaching and modeling what radically inclusive love and hospitality look like
- Showing compassion for those who are hurt, broken, and marginalized
- Being a builder of the beloved community
- Helping us increase our capacity to envision and embody life as multicultural, multiethnic, and multigenerational communities
- Not giving in to shame or timidity
- Responding to God's call not to be careful but to be faithful
- Leading with humble courage.

Keep Working

"So don't be ashamed of the testimony about the Lord or of me. . . . He destroyed death and brought life and immortality into clear focus through the good news. . . . Protect this good thing that has been placed in your trust" (2 Timothy 1:8-14 CEB).

William Sloane Coffin, in his book *The Collected Sermons by William Sloane Coffin,* speaks eloquently about proactively guarding and upholding the faith in the world:

> There is no way that Christianity can be spiritually redemptive without being socially responsible. . . . God is always trying to make humanity more human. But without us he won't, and without him we can't.[3]

Similarly, John Wesley taught: Solitary religion is not to be found there. . . . The gospel of Christ knows of no religion, but social; no holiness but social holiness. Faith working by love, is the length and breadth and depth and height of Christian perfection.[4]

As we encounter and engage the sometimes acrimonious disputes over issues of sexual practice and ethnics, the nature of marriage and the consecration of Christian ministry; as we hear news of actions and reactions across the UM connection, with rulings and declarations, reactions of affirmation and of rebuttal, we recognize first and foremost that in this turmoil and disruption, there are no winners.

Dr. Martin Luther King, Jr. described our situation perfectly, saying, "We are all caught in an inescapable network of mutuality, tied in a single garment of destiny. Whatever affects one directly, affects all indirectly." King also said, "I can never be what I ought to be until you are what you ought to be."[5]

We are the beloved community of Christ. When one part of the body hurts and suffers, we all hurt and suffer. We must pray and then work to assure that we will stay the course and not grow weary in doing good.

We are called to be steadfast in the face of adversity, fear, and division. We trust in God for the stamina and persistence to not lose heart or abandon hope, to stay focused and intent on advancing the mission of the church.

What's Next?

Animated by the power of the Spirit, bold in our witness, and committed to our shared labor together, let's invest in the work of bearing witness to unity for the sake of the gospel of Jesus Christ. I urge you my sisters and my brothers to stay the course, upholding one another in three essential endeavors:

1. Celebrating and expanding our diverse and global family, engaged in the shared mission of making disciples of Jesus Christ for the transformation of the world.
2. Learning and striving to improve the ways we joyfully choose the difficult but important path we walk in order to live together, embracing our dissimilarities with respect and without presuming or requiring that we will resolve all our differences.
3. Discerning how to share in the witness of our church that in courageous unity empowers all without exception to know and share the love of Christ. We are sinners, yet we rely on grace and encourage one another as we seek to do the work of peace in a world in which we must learn to accept diversity of thought as well as of practice.

Together we will find our way forward proclaiming and becoming God's beloved community. We grow in our relationship with Christ and in deeper relationships with one another when we sit at the table together and participate in meaningful and respectful dialogue. As we humbly share our different perspectives and draw from our unique experiences, we come to see one another as gifted and blessed children of our loving, forgiving, and generous God.

As we prepare to receive and reflect upon the findings of the Commission on a Way Forward and the Council of Bishops, we recognize that creating the beloved and faithful community by loving God and neighbor with our whole heart, mind, and soul is the work of a faithful and obedient church.

As United Methodists, we know the power of prayer and the transforming work of holy conferencing. Every United Methodist, every congregation, and every annual conference is invited and needed as a faithful partner in the journey ahead.

These are acrimonious, too often fuming, and anxious times. We can do better. We must do better. For we are the heirs of Susanna and John Wesley, Martin Luther King, Jr., James Thomas, Leontyne Kelley, and Jesse DeWitt. And now is the time for you and me to help prepare the way for the outpouring of God's love and redemptive work in the world.

May the Spirit of God continue to take up residence in our lives and lead us to places we have not dared to go, to people we have not dared to meet, to love where we have shown no love before, and to do good where we've shown no mercy.

NOTES

1. "Baptismal Covenant I," *The United Methodist Hymnal* (Nashville: The United Methodist Publishing House, 1989), 34.
2. Paraphrased, see statement at http://www.umc.org/news-and-media/council-of-bishops-names-32-commission-members. Accessed November 17, 2017.
3. William Sloane Coffin, "Being Called," in *The Collected Sermons of William Sloane Coffin: The Riverside Years, Volume 1* (Louisville: Westminster John Knox Press, 2008), 463.
4. John Wesley, *Hymns and Sacred Poems* [1739], Preface, page viii.
5. Dr. Martin Luther King, Jr., "Remaining Awake Through a Great Revolution," Commencement Address for Oberlin College, June, 1965, Oberlin Ohio; http://www2.oberlin.edu/external/EOG/BlackHistoryMonth/MLK/CommAddress.html. Accessed November 17, 2017.

12

Walking on Water

Donna Pritchard

Donna Pritchard is senior pastor, First United Methodist Church of Portland, Oregon.

WHEN I RETURNED HOME TO PORTLAND, Oregon, following the first meeting of The United Methodist Bishops' Commission on a Way Forward, a friend asked me to describe the purpose and goal of the commission's work. When I quoted a portion of the mission statement given to us by the Council of Bishops—to "design a way for being church that maximizes the presence of a United Methodist witness in as many places in the world as possible, that allows for as much contextual differentiation as possible, and that balances an approach to different theological understandings of human sexuality with a desire for as much unity as possible"[1]—he laughed, then commented, "Great! And after you do that, maybe you could just take a little stroll across the Columbia River!"

Faced with the complexity of our task, and given the depth of the positional divides we have created within the church for decades, this work of unity in diversity does at times feel as if we are attempting to walk on water. Yet we cannot simply cower in the bottom of the boat while the waves of social change and cultural conflicts batter us from all sides. Jesus is clearly calling to us in the midst of the storm, and the question is whether we will have the courage to step out of our preconceived notions of "church" in order to follow him.

Recently, theologian Jürgen Moltmann suggested, "Anyone who trusts the living God does not just see the world in terms of its reality. Realists do that and they always arrive too late. Anyone who trusts the future sees the world according to its potential."[2] The world relies upon us Christ-followers to see its full potential in the light of the gospel. As Wesleyan Christians, we cannot separate our love for God from our passion to create the kind of world where God's kin-dom can truly be incarnated here on this earth. It is our theological and practical task to please God as the prophet Micah instructs, "to do justice, and to love kindness, and to walk humbly with your God" (Micah 6:8 NRSV).

I am privileged to serve God in collaboration with the people of the First United Methodist Church (and indeed, the first church of any kind) in Portland, Oregon. This congregation has been advocating for social justice, caring for community needs, and attending to spiritual growth since 1848, three years before Portland itself was incorporated. In 1993, they made the decision to become one of the first seventy-five "Reconciling Congregations," based on a conviction that God's inclusive love demands the full inclusion of all persons in the life of the Church. As the lead pastor, I regularly witness an extraordinary openness and graciousness extended not only to members of the LGBTQIA community, but also to people who are without homes, people who are living below the poverty level, people with handicapping conditions, and people with mental illness. I believe the congregation's ability to welcome and embrace others began and is undergirded by their commitment to the full inclusion of their gay, lesbian, bisexual, transgender, queer, intersex and asexual neighbors. These United Methodists understand radical hospitality and full inclusion is essential to the work of doing justice, loving kindness, and walking humbly with God.

For every United Methodist congregation similarly committed to the full inclusion of LGBTQIA persons, there are others who insist on maintaining restrictions they see as preserving traditional values and protecting the theological integrity of the denomination. Good United Methodists differ greatly in their opinions about God's preferred future for the church in this regard, yet most would agree we can no longer navigate our great divide without doing serious harm to one another and to the mission of the church.

We are not alone in this struggle. The human community and even creation itself is being tossed about in very stormy seas right now (think global climate change, political and religious violence resulting in mass migration and population displacement, widespread economic injustice, as well as struggles around LGBTQIA equality). Jesus is calling to us in the midst of the storm, and we cannot pretend that our little United Methodist boat is not leaking. We cannot see the world only as it is, and thereby risk arriving too late. Nor can we turn deaf ears and blind eyes to Jesus' invitation to step out of our boat, walk across the water, and help to change the world. We will not make it very far, however, if we insist on walking alone. Like Peter in Matthew 14:22-33, we must keep our eyes on Jesus. Like the early Methodists, we will find our strength in one another. Placing a high priority on our relationships across the global United Methodist connection is critical if we are to see and co-create the world according to its gospel potential.

Margaret Wheatley, a management consultant who studies organizational behavior, writes, "Relationships are all there is. Everything in the universe only exists because it is in relationship to everything else. Nothing exists in isolation. We have to stop pretending we are individuals who can go it alone."[3] Wheatley's wisdom seems to inspire this description of the scope of work given to the Commission on a Way Forward, in which the Council of Bishops tells us:

> We should be open to new ways of embodying unity that move us beyond where we are in the present impasse and cycle of action and reaction around ministry and human sexuality. Therefore, we should consider *new ways of being in relationship across cultures and jurisdictions,* in understandings of episcopacy, in contextual definitions of autonomy for annual conferences, and in the design and purpose of the apportionment.[4]

Relationship is key to all of human existence. Relationship is central to Christian faith. Prioritizing relationships across the jurisdictions and the cultures of United Methodism is vital if we are to find ways to partner in our mission of making disciples for Jesus Christ and transforming the world.

Again, in Wheatley's words: "In order to counter the negative organizational dynamics stimulated by stress and uncertainty, we must give full attention to the quality of our relationships. Nothing else works, no new tools or technical applications, no redesigned organizational chart. *The solution is each other.* If we can rely on one another, we can cope with almost anything. Without each other, we retreat into fear."[5]

The solution is one another. Twyla Tharp also sees the value of prioritizing relationships. She has spent her career as a dancer and choreographer working with others, and she points out the life lessons learned through collaboration. She writes: "You need a challenging partner. In a good collaboration, differences between partners mean that one plus one will always equal more than two . . . [and] a great partnership is a lab where change happens every day."[6]

We United Methodists need one another. We need one another locally, and we need one another around the globe. We need to be challenged by differences in culture, language, skin color, economic status, profession, geography, scriptural interpretation, theology, experiences of God—by all the differences that shape our personal identities and our practice of ministry.

Ours can be a great partnership, one that supports, encourages, and creates the conditions for change every day. But if those who disagree with us depart from us, or if we choose to "take our game and go our own way," we will lose countless opportunities to grow. We will lose the richness that comes through diversity. We will be forever impoverished. And, perhaps most tragically, we will have given up on an incredible chance to model for the world its full potential in light of the gospel of Jesus Christ.

For too many years we seem to have been hanging on, hoping that folks would stop rocking the boat, when in fact the boat has been slowly filling with resentment, distrust, suspicion, and even hate. It will take all of us working together to empty the boat and begin to use it once more to reach our destination of God's beloved community on earth. We will only be able to do that by deciding that people matter more than positions and that relationships have priority over opinions—even scholarly opinions, even deeply held theological doctrines.

Prioritizing relationships in this way will require a leap of faith for all of us. We will need to risk trusting those who agree with us and those with whom we disagree on issues of same-gender relationships and related church practices. In order to embody this new kind of unity, complete with contextual autonomy for annual conferences to be most effective in each of their own mission fields, we will have to trust that the freedom given to the other is the same freedom returned to us. This will require a leap of faith no less profound or rewarding than the leap of faith required to get Peter out of the boat in response to Jesus' invitation. It is surely a leap worth taking. David Whyte, in his poem entitled "The Truelove," paints a picture for us of just this kind of faithful leap—a willingness to grasp the "one hand you know/belongs in yours."[7]

After all our struggle and all these years, surely The United Methodist Church has had enough of drowning. Surely we want to live and we want to love enough to walk across the dangers of this present moment, trusting that we will be held by God's love and encouraged by Christ's presence. In 2017, perhaps more than at any other time in the history of our Church, the world needs us. It needs both our acts of piety and our acts of mercy. And the world needs all of us working together to realize its fullest potential in the light of God's gospel. Let us not arrive too late. Let us step out of the boat, together.

NOTES

1. Council of Bishops, The United Methodist Church, July, 2016.
2. From a speech before the General Council of the World Communion of Reformed Churches, June 30, 2017; http://wcrc.ch/news/the-living-god-challenges-death-and-destruction-jurgen-moltmann-tells-global-gathering-of-reformed-churches. Accessed November 19, 2017.
3. Margaret J. Wheatley, *Turning to One Another: Simple Conversations to Restore Hope to the Future* (San Francisco: Barrett-Koehler Publishers, 2009), 23.

4. Council of Bishops, The United Methodist Church, July 2016 (emphasis added); http://www.umc.org/who-we-are/commission-on-a-way-forward-about-us. Accessed November 19, 2017.
5. Margaret Wheatley, *When Change Is Out of Our Control,* Human Resources for the 21st Century (Wiley, 2003); http://www.margaretwheatley.com/articles/whenchangeisoutofcontrol.html. Accessed November 19, 2017.
6. Twyla Tharp, *The Collaborative Habit: Life Lessons for Working Together* (New York: Simon & Schuster, 2009), 36, 40.
7. David Whyte, "The Truelove," in *River Flow: New and Selected Poems"* (Langley, Washington: Many Rivers Press, 2012), 198–200.

13

Before All Else

Kimberly D. Reisman

Kimberly D. Reisman is Executive Director, World Methodist Evangelism.

God Is Bigger

PAUL'S OPENING WORD TO THE Corinthians provides a vivid reminder for me in my work with World Methodist Evangelism. Before addressing the important issues of faith facing that fledgling church, he makes it clear that the church of Jesus Christ is much greater than this one group of followers:

> To the church of God that is in Corinth, to those who are sanctified in Christ Jesus, called to be saints, ***together with all those who in every place call on the name of our Lord Jesus Christ***, both their Lord and ours: Grace to you and peace from God our Father and the Lord Jesus Christ. (1 Corinthians 1:2-3 NRSV, emphasis added)

Whatever the challenges the Corinthian church was facing, and there were many, Paul seems to have believed this bigger perspective was important enough to be mentioned before all else. As Christians, both within and beyond the Methodist Wesleyan family, we are sanctified in Christ Jesus, called to be saints, together with all those who in *every place* call on the name of our Lord Jesus Christ. We do not serve a provincial God, a God of one place. We do not serve a God limited to our own corner of the world, or constrained by our own experience of culture. Our God is God of the *whole world,* the God who both transcends and redeems culture, time, and place. When we join in this God's mission, we join *all* those who in *every* place call on the name of the Lord Jesus Christ.

This is especially meaningful to the work of World Methodist Evangelism, and I believe it is important to remember in any conversation about how to live with grace and respect within our Wesleyan tradition.[1] The global Methodist Wesleyan movement is indeed a family of Christians who call on the name of the Lord Jesus Christ in every place. We are over 80 million strong, scattered across 130 different countries. We are like a rain forest whose trees have intertwining roots. Our roots grow deep into the soil not only of the movement launched by John Wesley, but also of the church universal across the centuries. And our branches grow upward and outward in a great and varied canopy that stretches across the planet on which God has scattered us. In the United Methodist branch of this Wesleyan Methodist family tree, there are over 12 million of us scattered across 58 different countries.[2] We grow from those same roots and are a vital part of that same canopy.

The Wesleyan Methodist canopy is varied for many reasons, one of which is the assortment of expressions of church. Some, like the United Methodist branch, have an episcopacy (including, in some places, archbishops!), but others do not. Some, like the United Methodist branch, have itinerant clergy, yet others do not. Some, like the United Methodist branch, are tightly connected, while others hold the connectional reigns more loosely. Nevertheless, though our canopy may be varied, our roots in the universal church enable us, amidst this varied structure, to call upon the name of the Lord Jesus Christ, Messiah, Son of the Triune God, the One who transcends, heals, and redeems the entire world. And it is our roots, not our canopy, that empower us to join God's healing, transforming mission of salvation for all the world.

Recognizing that as Christians in the Wesleyan tradition, it is not our canopy but our roots that connect us to one another in Christ leads us to an even deeper realization: God has blessed the church with more spiritual gifts, greater wisdom, mightier courage, deeper spiritual insight, stronger commitment to prayer, more profound holiness, more absolute trust, and more expansive joy than any one language or culture can contain on its own. It is this truth that guides us as we navigate the inevitable disagreements that arise within a global family. It is this truth that calls us to the humility necessary for any follower of Jesus—a humility grounded in the knowledge that our understanding will always be limited by our own culture and experience.

This humility is crucial to living with grace and respect in our Wesleyan tradition, even amid disagreement, and it is especially important when it comes to evangelism. That is because evangelism must precede all internal disagreements, whatever they might be. Humility empowers us to recognize that.

Our Way of Being[3]

One way that helps me grasp the humility necessary to share the gospel with integrity and to live with grace and respect is through a metaphor. Metaphors are helpful because they point to ideas that are often deeper than words alone can convey. In this case, the metaphor of *embrace* moves us closer to understanding the crucial element of humility. When we visualize an embrace, we can see that it consists of four integrated stages: we open our arms, we wait, we close our arms, and finally we open them again. Without all four, an embrace is not complete. There is much that can be said about the metaphor of embrace; however, in this context, it is the first part—when we open our arms—that is significant. This first stage provides a vivid illustration of the stance of humble openness that should ground the way we Christians carry ourselves in the world.

As Christians, we believe in the one God of Abraham. We believe that because of God's promise to Abraham, *all* of humanity will receive God's blessings. Through Abraham, all the families of the earth will be blessed. N. T. Wright calls this God's "covenant-with-Abraham-for-the-blessing-of-all." This covenant points to God's plan to redeem the all-encompassing condition of estrangement that affects every human being.[4] And yet right now, there are many people missing from that divinely promised one family of Abraham.

When we open our arms to initiate embrace, we are conveying our recognition of that void. We are signaling our desire that the void be filled, and we have made space within ourselves for others to enter so that the one family of Abraham might be complete. At the same time we convey that we have made space, our open arms also communicate that we are reaching out—softly knocking on the other person's door, so to speak. They express the reality that the boundaries that make up the divinely promised one family of Abraham are permeable, and our movement is in two directions.

Cultivating the humility necessary for both evangelism and living with grace and respect involves recognizing the brokenness and woundedness that marks all human life. This too is conveyed by the opening of our arms. Because the world is wounded, it will never be completely as we would like it to be; and yet, the space created when we extend our open arms reflects our understanding that we are no more immune to that brokenness than anyone else. They indicate that though we recognize the estrangement that marks being human, we would rather reach out than continue that estrangement.

Because the world will never be completely as we would like it to be, a stance of humility in the face of human brokenness is vital. It should mark our way of being in the world as followers of Christ. It should mark our way of being in the world as we reach out to those beyond the boundaries of our faith communities. And it should mark our way of being in the world as we seek to live with grace and respect amid disagreement. It is this stance that undergirds everything we do.

Before All Else

Following Jesus with a posture of humble openness leads us to recognize a significant truth: Some things cannot be said until after other things are said.[5] This was sage advice given to me by a cherished mentor. We open our arms, reaching out to others before anything and everything else. Before judgment, before confession, before forgiveness, even before the resolution of any and all of our internal disagreements.

Jesus' story of the prodigal son in Luke 15 helps illustrate this. When the son comes to himself and begins his journey home, the father is already waiting for him on the road. Before the son has an opportunity to do anything—confess, ask for forgiveness, or be taken back as a hired hand—the father's arms are already open and the son is gathered to him in embrace. The son begins his journey home with a vision of himself as unworthy to be called his father's son and only to be received as a hired hand, but his father's open arms and subsequent embrace transform him into "this son of mine."

As with many of Jesus' stories, there is more than one important figure. The story of the prodigal is no exception. Not only is there a lesson related to the younger, returning son, there is a lesson related to the older son as well. The contrast between the response of the father and the response of the older son is significant, both for evangelism and for discerning how to live with grace and respect amidst disagreement.

For the father, his younger son's return was paramount. He was willing to reach out, before anything and everything else. He knew the importance of confession, which is why he allowed his son the opportunity to admit that he had sinned. He knew his son would need to face the full consequences of his actions in order to be transformed, which is why he was generous in offering a ring, but not a new inheritance. And yet, the order of these experiences is clearly the father's chief concern. The welcome back is of utmost importance. The son's understanding of himself as beloved was the understanding that needed to be realized first, before all else.

The older son's response is quite a contrast. For him, it was the prodigal's sin that was first and foremost. So blinding was the prodigal's sin that the older brother could no longer recognize him as his brother; rather, in conversation with his father, the prodigal becomes "this son of yours." While the father understood the welcome to take priority in the order of transformation, the older brother placed the prodigal's sin before all else, and as a result, was unable to welcome him at all.

The father understood my mentor's advice that some things cannot be said until other things are said. This guided how he related to both of his sons. Just as the prodigal needed to understand that he was beloved before any transformation could take place, the same was true for the older brother. When he responds to his older son, before explaining anything, he insists that the older brother is always with him and everything he has is his. The older brother remains beloved as he always has been, and that love is not diminished by the return of the younger son.

Because the Wesleyan Methodist family is global, there will always be points of disagreement. Specific branches in our family may encounter internal discord as well. But even as we seek to live with grace and respect in that context, there is a greater reality that should weigh even heavier on our shoulders as followers of Jesus Christ. The promised one family of Abraham is not yet complete. Estrangement and brokenness abound. The world is not as we would like it to be, nor as God intended it to be. And yet, as those who in every place call on the name of the Lord Jesus Christ, we must recognize that though our God is not limited by culture or place, we are; and that limitation requires that we approach the world with humble openness. With a willingness to open our arms, to create space within ourselves and reach out, before anything and everything else. In this way, we make room for the power of the Holy Spirit to work within us, within others, and between us and others, so that forgiveness can be received and given, reconciliation and healing can be experienced, and transformation can begin.

NOTES

1. World Methodist Evangelism falls under the missional umbrella of the World Methodist Council. WME works within the global Methodist Wesleyan family (of which The United Methodist Church is one part among many) to empower individuals and congregations for holistic evangelism, discipleship, and leadership development.

2. "Central Conferences," http://www.umc.org/who-we-are/central-conferences; "Data Services," http://www.gcfa.org/data-services. Accessed November 19, 2017.
3. The discussion of our "way of being" is based on World Methodist Evangelism's resource, *Embrace: The Essence of Authentic Evangelism*, Kimberly D. Reisman (Franklin: Seedbed, publication pending).
4. N. T. Wright, "First-Century Judaism: Covenant, Law and Lawcourt," in *Justification: God's Plan and Paul's Vision* (Downers Grove: IVP Academic, 2009), 55–77; especially 67.
5. William J. Abraham, personal conversation.

14

Unity as Witness

Laceye Warner

Laceye Warner is Associate Professor of the Practice of Evangelism and Methodist Studies, Duke Divinity School.

THE INTEGRITY OF The United Methodist Church's Christian witness is at stake in the midst of the enduring disagreements regarding same-gender relationships and related church practices. By this I do not mean The UMC's witness is at stake because of contrary practices of either the "orthodox" or "progressives" related to a particular interpretation of Scripture regarding human sexuality and ecclesial privileges. Rather, The UMC's Christian witness is at stake due to the manner in which individuals and groups on opposing sides have characterized and interacted with one another. From my perspective as a mid-career faculty member in a university-related theological school teaching courses in United Methodist studies and mission/evangelism, there is more at stake in these decisions than the logistics of polity (including the implications of which side might "win"), but rather our identity and life together not only as United Methodists, but as Christians in the body of Christ. This essay draws from United Methodist Doctrinal Standards to argue that church unity is a means of grace and Christian witness. Regardless of whether each side perceives the other's actions or beliefs as sinful, schism is sinful. When practiced as a means of grace, unity offers a Christian witness to God's unfolding reign.

Missional Means of Grace

Scholars have asserted that the early Methodist movement—above all else—was evangelistic. While other denominational traditions often trace their roots to disagreements regarding confessional or theological points, the Wesleyan tradition emerged from an evangelistic and missional imperative. For many this missional evangelistic character at the core of United Methodist identity is a powerful attribute shaping Methodism. Yet, how does this attribute complement—and at times contrast with—a perceived deficiency in our identity; namely, an ambiguous ecclesiology?

The nature of The United Methodist Church can seem elusive. United Methodist ecclesiology holds in creative and competing tension preceding traditions—including Anglican, Catholic, and Puritan. Albert Outler's question, "Do Methodists have a doctrine of the Church?" echoes and sometimes haunts conversations regarding Methodist ecclesiology. Outler offers an accurate, but ambiguous, response, "The answer 'yes' says too much; 'no' says too little. 'In a manner of speaking,' which is more nearly accurate than the other two, seems nevertheless equivocal."[1]

Richard Heitzenrater responds to Outler's question by describing the church as a *means of grace*. Heitzenrater's response is an effort to align the being of the church, or what it "is," and the practices of the church, or what it "does."[2] The means of grace in Wesleyan tradition acknowledge the presence and accessibility of God's grace for those participating in individual and communal practices. Means of grace function to bring humanity closer to God and closer to one another. Schism is antithetical to the function of the means of grace. The church is the primary location in which one lives out one's faith, as a participant in a community of faith and member of the body of Christ. From the proclamation of the gospel to its embodiment in lives and communities, the church at its best functions as a means of God's grace (see Scott J. Jones, *United Methodist Doctrine: The Extreme Center* [Nashville: Abingdon Press, 2002; 255]).

The United Methodist Church's character as a means of grace includes the practice of its organization and polity. While still human, and therefore fallible, throughout history the formation of the denomination's structure has kept its missional purpose at the center. For example, the structure of annual conferences, the episcopacy, the itineracy, ordination, and general boards may be understood as prudential means of grace[3]—and means of participating in God's sanctification of individuals and communities in God's unfolding reign. For John Wesley, prudential means of grace included Christian conferencing, even and perhaps especially when attendees worked through disagreements as the body of Christ. The United Methodist Church's character as a prudential means of grace also includes its polity, ministry—and unity.

The UMC has presumed a more highly structured ecclesiology than its theological imperative demands, leading to the increasing and disproportionate attention by the highest bodies of the church to issues beyond the constitutionally protected doctrinal standards, including the issue of human sexuality. In such an imbalance, questions of human sexuality (and arguably other questions of social ethics) receive much more attention by these bodies than significant aspects of the denomination's constitutionally protected doctrinal standards.

Doctrinal Standards and Unity

United Methodism's doctrinal standards include the Articles of Religion appropriated by John Wesley and the Confession of Faith from the Evangelical United Brethren. Both documents include articles on "The Church." Attention is largely given to the early Articles of Religion statement: "Article XIII—Of the Church," which reads:

The visible church of Christ is a congregation of faithful men in which the pure Word of God is preached, and the Sacraments duly administered according to Christ's ordinance, in all those things that of necessity are requisite to the same (*The Book of Discipline of The United Methodist Church, 2016,* par. 104, p. 68).

However, the article from the EUB Confession of Faith draws directly from Scripture, describing the church as "***one***, holy, apostolic and catholic" (*Book of Discipline, 2016,* par. 104, p. 73, emphasis added). When these scriptural ecclesial themes receive attention through the Wesleyan doctrinal frames of sanctification and the means of grace, the practice of church unity—not merely church conferencing—emerges as a means of grace and important component of Christian witness.

One way to understand the level of authority granted to specific doctrinal standards within United Methodism is to consider the difficulty and complexity of the process required to alter them. As the Constitution of The United Methodist Church establishes, and upon which the *Discipline* expands in more detail, the General Conference is the only authoritative body empowered to speak for the denomination. In balance, the Restrictive Rules, first implemented in 1808 with the first Constitution by The Methodist Episcopal Church, restrict the activity of the General Conference through constraints on that power. With regard to doctrinal authority, the Restrictive Rules prevent the General Conference from revising, adding, or deleting doctrinal standards without a three-fourths approving vote of the aggregate number of annual conference members.

The doctrinal standards possessing the highest level of authority may be referred to as "constitutional standards." These include the Articles of Religion (protected by the first Restrictive Rule), Confession of Faith (protected by the second Restrictive Rule), General Rules (protected by the fifth Restrictive Rule), and the Constitution. Though our constitutional standards are clearly distinct from one another in substance, they share authority both in their protection by the Constitution as well as in their significance for the constancy of teaching within the Methodist tradition. The Constitution and General Rules may only be changed with a two-thirds approving vote of the annual conference members. Notably, there has been no vote or action within The Methodist Episcopal Church, or traditions stemming from it, to revise the constitutionally protected doctrinal standards, including the General Rules.

The Articles of Religion and Evangelical United Brethren Confession of Faith (as well as John Wesley's General Rules) are formally recognized as doctrine of The United Methodist Church, protected by the Constitution and Restrictive Rules, and serve as doctrinal foundations. The first Restrictive

Rule also refers to "our present existing and established standards of doctrine" (*Discipline,* par. 17, p. 31). The interpretation of this latter clause is disputed, and its meaning continues to provoke debate. A rationale based on the *Discipline,* specifically "Our Doctrinal Heritage," claims this clause includes Wesley's *Standard Sermons* and his *Explanatory Notes upon the New Testament* (*Discipline,* par. 103, p. 64). Richard Heitzenrater argues that the phrase covers only the Articles of Religion (*Discipline,* par. 103, p. 59). Bishop Jones argues that the General Conference is the only authoritative arbiter of this discussion, and the General Conference has decided the *Sermons* and *Notes* are included as doctrinal standards. According to the *Discipline,* "Within the Wesleyan tradition, then as now, the *Sermons* and *Notes* furnished models of doctrinal exposition" (*Discipline,* par. 103, p. 60). According to this statement, these texts, with those explicitly named, carry the weight of tradition.

Interestingly, despite the latter ambiguity as well as numerous other questions and conflicts, as mentioned above, the constitutionally protected doctrinal standards have not been revised. Considerable time has been invested by individuals, delegations, interest groups, task forces, boards, and agencies composing legislation and managing revisions of aspects of the *Discipline* related to the issue of human sexuality, among many other issues. This is not unexpected, and it can be faithful work. While our doctrinal standards have not been revised, they have at times been arguably undermined by such efforts, particularly when intentionally or unintentionally ignored. To address difficult issues without sufficiently attending to our historically and deeply held beliefs and practices neglects the gifts of our heritage and undermines our Christian witness.

Unity as Witness

For early Christians, such as the Orthodox of the Byzantine era, unity was the church's highest practice of Christian witness: missional witness to the ***one***, holy, apostolic church.[4] Though the Orthodox tradition has been critiqued by many for equating the kingdom of God on earth with the visible (Orthodox) church gathering, these emphases offer helpful complements to

Western evangelical influences. Instead of emphasizing the centrifugal, or mission-as-going-out, Orthodox perspectives on mission emphasize the centripetal dynamic of mission—specifically, the witness of the gathered worshiping community.[5] The eucharistic liturgy with its missional structure and purpose embodies an act of witness.[6] Following the Great Schism of 1054 Roman Catholicism, followed by Protestantism, through individuals, orders, and organizations persisted in centrifugal missionary outreach. The Orthodox, however, understood its purpose, or mission, as a pursuit of Christian unity, unity lost as a result of the division in 1054.[7]

The urgency of the Great Commission, which United Methodism shares, did not occur until the late eighteenth century. For most, including Martin Luther and John Calvin, the apostles fulfilled Jesus' final commissions recorded in the Gospels so that the tasks described in these texts were generally considered complete by Christian communities and interpreters of Scripture. The Gospel commissions continue to guide contemporary Christians in fulfilling our baptismal commissions to share the gospel in our words and in our lives; specifically, "to accept God's grace for themselves, to profess their faith openly, and to lead a Christian life."[8] United Methodists and other mainline Protestants in the U.S. tend not to consider church unity as an aspect of Christian witness. This is not surprising in light of the history of Protestantism in the U.S. as disestablished communities in a young nation practicing democracy and free market principles of consumer-driven capitalism. Some scholars note that schism among U.S. Protestants at times increases overall participation and could therefore, albeit ironically, be considered evangelistic.

Unity as described in Scripture, the creeds, and included in United Methodist doctrinal standards is a mystery of our shared faith. Too often conversations about and efforts surrounding unity default to human and fallible terms (a Pelagian tendency not unfamiliar to John Wesley's Methodism or ours). Similar to other Christian doctrines in which the human and divine agencies interact (sanctification, for example), unity as a means of grace is sacred space that hopes for the eschatologically not yet—as a gift of God's grace—in the midst of the fallible space of the already. May United Methodists, and all Christians, pray for and with God's grace work toward an eschatological hope for unity.

Witness as *Imitatio Dei*

The most pressing questions of faith are not specifically about human sexuality or other ethical "issues." Rather, the pressing question is, "Will we receive the Triune God's unconditional love and redemption that restores relationships, unity, with God, others, and creation?" Do the narratives, language, practices, and traditions over time of our ecclesial community(-ies) reflect the gift of the Triune God's love—which cannot be earned, but only received? United Methodism is in great need of the forgiveness and restoration necessary to fully participate in witness as *imitatio Dei*. As we continue to work out our salvation through pursuing the means of grace and our shared sanctification of God's work in us, then we may know oneness and unity with God, others, and creation that is eschatological.

An example demonstrating the eschatological possibility of unity, even with such a difficult issue as human sexuality, is a local UM congregation my spouse served many years ago. This local church was historically Swedish Methodist before later becoming United Methodist. As the diversity in the surrounding geographic area increased, a long-serving and beloved pastor began welcoming first-generation immigrants into the congregation. The new members—some from Belize, Jamaica, and Haiti, some living in group homes with special needs, and some with no homes at all—were welcomed by this pastor and took their places in the leadership of the local church. While those welcomed by this pastor generally represented a much more conservative theology than the progressive pastor who ministered to them, the congregation—then mostly populated by first-generation African-Caribbean members—deeply loved him and respected his leadership.

When he was diagnosed with late-stage cancer, the congregation was overcome with grief. On his deathbed, the pastor made a difficult request of his theologically conservative congregation—to become what was then referred to as a "Reconciling Congregation" and to welcome a group of mostly gay men into the congregation. This even more diverse congregation would retain very different views on the issue of human sexuality. However, the beloved pastor, who had loved people across boundaries, allowed those once-new members to also love across boundaries. Subsequently, the congregation welcomed others, including the group of primarily gay men, into the congregation, its leadership roles, homes, and hearts. The local church was never of one mind on the issue of human sexuality and was likely the most conservative Reconciling Congregation in the denomination, but they embodied eschatological hope of the unity of the body of Christ as they celebrated God's gift of the not-yet in the midst of the already.

The lingering possibility of schism among United Methodists not only saddens many, but also undermines our long-held and deeply rooted missional character and Christian witness. With the richness of our doctrinal heritage, this seems especially distressing. We are allowing an issue, while very significant, to rupture the unity of United Methodism—the eschatological hope included among the denomination's doctrinal standards. Though it may be too late for restoration in our lifetime, my hope and prayer is that the richness of United Methodism's doctrinal standards, structure, and missional purpose offers an opportunity to weather this storm that continues to rip through other mainline Protestant denominations. May United Methodism, among many others, practice unity as a means of grace, witnessing to God's unfolding reign.

NOTES

1. Albert C. Outler, "Do Methodists Have a Doctrine of the Church?" in *The Wesleyan Theological Heritage*, ed. Thomas C. Oden and Leicester R. Longden (Grand Rapids: Zondervan, 1991), 212.

2. Richard Heitzenrater, "Wesleyan Ecclesiology: Methodism as a Means of Grace," in *Orthodox and Wesleyan Ecclesiology*, ed. S. T. Kimbrough Jr. (Crestwood, NY: St. Vladimir's Press, 2007), 119–28.
3. Scott J. Jones, *United Methodist Doctrine: The Extreme Center* (Nashville: Abingdon Press, 2002), 255.
4. See David Bosch, *Transforming Mission: Paradigm Shifts in Theology of Mission* (Maryknoll, NY: Orbis Books, 1991), 208.
5. Ibid., 207–208.
6. Ibid., 208.
7. Ibid.
8. "Baptismal Covenant I," *The United Methodist Hymnal* (Nashville: The United Methodist Publishing House, 1989), 34.

15

Shameless Spirituality: Sharing the Gospel in a Season of Suspicion and Separation

Audrey Warren

Audrey Warren is senior pastor, First United Methodist Church of Miami.

"OUR FIRST PRACTICE TOGETHER, I cried the entire time. I don't know why, but I cried." These were the words of one of our longtime choir members, reflecting on the first choir practice she attended when her church merged with the church across the street. In November 2016, I had the immense joy of celebrating with this unified congregation one hundred and twenty years of joint history and ministry in downtown Miami. I have learned much. Their stories have informed my historical understanding of the church and have given me some insight as to how The United Methodist Church might live into a future amid a season of deep suspicion and whispers of separation.

I sat with members and recorded their stories for a documentary we made to celebrate our 120th anniversary. After hearing the stories over and again, a few themes began to emerge—a shameless attention to spiritualty and an openness to the creativity of the Holy Spirit. Could it be that The United Methodist Church bears witness to graceful and mutually respectful ways of living in the Wesleyan tradition amid enduring disagreements by embracing a shameless spirituality in sharing the gospel of Jesus Christ with the world and embracing the creative work of the Holy Spirit?

Shameless Spirituality

The term *shameless spirituality* has arisen in my heart as I have listened to the stories of pioneers of our church and of the city of Miami. One of the city's and the church's first pioneers was James Jackson, a doctor from West Palm Beach who was called upon in 1896 by Henry Flagler to be the doctor at the "hoped-for" train station in the "hoped-for" city of Miami. Dr. Jackson took a wagon to Fort Lauderdale and then hopped on a boat, which was the only way to get to Miami. He got off the boat on a rainy day, walked around the "city," and saw the wooden roads moving around in the mud. An hour later he walked back to the marina to return to Fort Lauderdale, as he had decided not to stay in such a primitive place. He arrived at the marina only to learn the next ride back was in two weeks. Within those two weeks he decided to remain in Miami. While some might say he had literally "missed the boat," others might describe his decision as accepting the adventure of a lifetime.

Dr. Jackson's first office/hospital was just a small room, yet he practiced medicine with excellence. His first church was a boat and included Presbyterians, Baptists, and Lutherans as well as Methodists. The structure of space, framework of worship, mode of music, and branch of denomination were not important. What was important was gathering together to worship God—even with the salty smell of fish hovering over the waters. What else was important was sharing the gospel with all the new people who moved to the strange town. Shameless spirituality is a spirit, mission, and calling to share the gospel of Jesus Christ without shame about lack of structure or the need to have all the answers. A shameless spirituality is one that holds on only to the pillars of our life together with God and one another. Shameless spirituality is sharing the gospel at all cost because you know you have nothing to lose if you are holding on to faith, hope, and love!

Paul speaks of this shameless spirituality in his letter to the Corinthians when he writes, "I have made myself a slave to everyone, to win as many as possible. To the Jews I became like a Jew, to win the Jews. To those under the law I became like one under the law (though I myself am not under the law), so as to win those under the law. To those not having the law I became like one not having the law (though I am not free from God's law but am under Christ's law), so as to win those not having the law. To the weak I became weak, to win the weak. I have become all things to all people so that by all possible means I might save some. I do all this for the sake of the gospel, that I may share in its blessings" 1 Corinthians 9:19-23 NIV). Paul speaks of putting aside his own preference and even modifying his own life for the purpose of sharing the gospel.

Spiritual Intelligence

The practice of shameless spirituality takes much spiritual intelligence. In 1995 Daniel Goleman made the term *emotional intelligence* part of our sociological dialogue. Emotional intelligence is the ability of individuals to recognize their own emotions as well as others' emotions and to manage emotions and be able to "persist in frustrations, to control the impulse and delay gratification; to regulate one's moods and keep distress from swamping the ability to think; to empathize and to hope."[1] Like emotional intelligence, spiritual intelligence is the ability of an individual to recognize and listen to what the Holy Spirit is speaking in any given situation as well as the ability to consider what the Holy Spirit might be saying to someone else.

Spiritual intelligence is being able to navigate a diversity of opinions and beliefs and discover together what the Spirit might be speaking. Bishop Ken Carter of the Florida Annual Conference has added to my understanding of spiritual intelligence by inviting all churches to differentiate between preferences and purpose. Although one's preference might be traditional worship or wooden pews, that preference might not help carry forward the purpose of sharing the gospel of Jesus Christ; and in some ways those preferences might even negatively affect the communication of the gospel.

Without doubt it is the spiritual intelligence or spiritual maturity of the members of First United Methodist Church of Miami that has kept them close to God's heart and surviving as a church in Miami when many others have closed. As Miami grew into a proper city, so churches also grew into "proper churches" with big buildings, powerful pipe organs, and crismons on their Christmas Trees. As one might imagine, buildings, finance, and leadership caused that early interdenominational boat church to split into its respective denominations. One of those became Trinity Methodist Episcopal Church South. A few years later, White Temple Methodist Episcopal Church was born just across the street.

Trinity and White Temple grew with the number of military bases in Miami Beach and the Keys, with worship attendance eventually reaching almost six thousand people between the two each Sunday. After the Methodist Episcopal Church and the Methodist Episcopal Church South united in 1939, these two congregations who met across the street from each other spoke for twenty-seven years about merging. It was not until a Saturday night in 1966 that White Temple caught fire, forcing the two churches to put aside their preferences of location, pastor, and political beliefs and come together with a common purpose in downtown Miami. Some still say, "The Holy Spirit did what we could not . . . bring us together." To say these words even fifty-one years after the fire takes a great deal of spiritual intelligence. The ones who tell these stories are now in their eighties. When the two churches merged these members were in their thirties, raising young children while doing the work of unification. The longtime choir member who cried at the first joint practice was one of those young mothers who volunteered for the church and sang in the choir. She still cannot explain her tears, but she remembers the early days as being hard work but worthy work.

The Creative Work of the Holy Spirit

This work required shameless spirituality as well as spiritual intelligence, but it also required an openness to the creative work of the Holy Spirit. Not only were the thirty-something young Christians charged with uniting with one another but also with an ever-growing diverse city and downtown. The same year the churches united, Congress passed the Cuban Adjustment Act, allowing Cuban exiles to have legal documentation in the United States. The church needed to find a way to connect with the growing Latino population.

A few years later the church built a new building and began to offer a Spanish service. By that time there were also many people migrating to downtown Miami from Caribbean countries. The church welcomed people of all skin colors and nationalities to be part of God's mission downtown.

The1980s were tumultuous years for downtown communities, and Miami was no different. City streets became beds by dusk for the homeless of downtown Miami. Once again FUMC Miami responded to its context and developed a ministry with homeless people. The younger generation of United Methodist Men proposed to the church council to start the Breakfast Club. The UMM would gather at 6:30 every Sunday morning and offer coffee and donuts to those who were homeless and then have a service in the fellowship hall for any who might want to stay. As one might imagine, letting over one hundred homeless men and women into a new church building was not received well by all. Yet, inspired by the Holy Spirit, the UMM asked if they could simply test it for a month. It proved to be an invaluable ministry to parishioner and homeless person alike.

Over the past forty years it is this very ministry that has attracted a diversity of people to FUMC. Local AA groups have become involved in the ministry, and many have become part of the church. The church has seen a large increase in the number of LGBTQ persons attending the church and becoming members. The first openly gay commissioner in Miami Dade County grew up at First Church. The church has always believed that anyone who wants to do God's work is welcome!

A time line of FUMC Miami shows that roughly every forty years, the church is being asked to look again at its context and reevaluate its mission field and its mission within. With the turn of the new millennium came a new downtown filled with high-rise condos, dog parks, and large concert venues. Once again First Church is being asked to use its spiritual imagination to dream with the Holy Spirit a new kind of church in a new downtown. In October 2015 the church began an exploratory process to redevelop the church property. After a year and a half of visioning, planning, and working with real estate professionals, the church voted in May 2017 to sell the property and rebuild at the same location—but integrated into a high-rise apartment tower built intentionally for social living. Leading the effort has been one of the United Methodist Men who is now in his eighties. He was also an architect for the new building the merged church built in 1980.

Throughout many conversations over two years I have been extremely impressed by the spiritual intelligence and trust in the Holy Spirit expressed by those who are now in their eighties. They are not concerned about where they will have their funeral but where the new people downtown will have to worship and find a faith community. Their decision to tear down their building was based not on their preference but on God's purpose. The church has taken the risk to listen deeply to its context and culture to hear where the creative work of the Holy Spirit might be leading, without compromising its mission in Miami.

Collapsing vs. Collaboration

As much as a church or individual might trust the creative work of the Holy Spirit, there is always fear. One fear that FUMC has expressed throughout our process of redevelopment is that of "blending in with the culture" physically, socially, and theologically. This is a fear that I have perceived is also expressed at a denominational level. We are not the first to have this fear; nor are we the first to flirt with the culture and context that surround us. In his book, *The Democratization of American Christianity,* former Wake Forest University president Nathan Hatch marks how American Christianity was influenced theologically and administratively by the revolutions and movements that created and sustained the United States in its early years of formation.[2]

Faith in America became individualized with a new focus on personal salvation shortly after the United States won its independence. Thomas Jefferson even created his own Bible by using a razor blade and glue and reconstructing the gospels as he saw fit within his naturalistic theology. Shortly after the United States imposed taxes, the Methodist Church created a system of apportionments. Culture has informed church for decades, and church has blended in with culture. Many can argue that the church must have some relationship with the culture in order to be relevant. It might help to distinguish between collapsing to the culture and collaborating with the culture.

Collapsing to the culture might require a complete compromising and even loss of beliefs, buildings, and traditions, but a collaboration with the culture might be more of an exchange of the best parts of each to benefit the whole. As FUMC Miami works toward the design of the new church building that will be integrated into a high rise, we are often tempted to go to battle for what we want. Yet over the past few months, we have come to recognize in our conversations with the developers and architects that many of our goals are similar. We do not have to collapse our imagery or ideas, but rather we get to collaborate about ways in which the church can offer the apartment portion welcome and vice versa. Together this creates a beautiful design as well as a church that is learning how to incarnate itself in a new world.

A Contextual Conclusion . . .

First United Methodist Church of Miami's ability to do the work of incarnation, which requires shameless spirituality, spiritual intelligence, and an openness to the creative work of the Holy Spirit will determine its future in downtown Miami. The same might be true of The United Methodist Church. Incarnational work does not happen at a macro level but rather at a micro level. Oddly enough, globalization and the technological revolution of the millennium have made the world not more generic but more diverse. As The United Methodist Church continues to find a way forward, I am drawn to the story of a small church in a big city—a church that defines itself not only by what it believes, but also by what it does and who it is within a community.

First Church Miami's story is simply one of countless stories that could be told about local churches throughout our connection, many of which have found ways to be shamelessly spiritual and to be available to the movement of the Holy Spirit in their context. The work for our denomination going forward must look to examples like these to understand that the work of the local church—which is the end to which our general conferences and annual conferences work—is best determined locally and contextually.

The issue is this: the tools of shameless spirituality that allow a local church to live fruitfully amid its diversity are best held in the space of a local incarnational context. The debate floors of General Conference and annual conferences have not demonstrated the ability to faithfully produce healthy and shameless spiritual tools that allow for fruitful focus on the mission field. Instead they have created division, distraction, and chaos. One might argue that the agenda of our governing conference is to provide governance for the church and not provide ministry strategies for the church. Wherever you stand, the sad reality is that our governing bodies are not providing either. The idea that we can have a one-size-fits-all understanding of something as complex as LGBTQ identity is idealistic at best.

Could it be that we should rather release local incarnational communities to discern what would propel them to contextually bear fruit in their mission field, while staying connected to the core essential doctrines of The United Methodist Church? We already allow deep contextualization that changes over time in our polity. The various forms of First Miami, from an interdenominational boat church to a divided church to a unified church to a church serving a Spanish-speaking neighborhood to a homeless-focused church to a church now part of an apartment tower: each movement shows evolving contextualization, much of which has been driven by the same faithful lay people who have stuck with the ship of this church despite the forays into uncharted territories.

Can our denomination not do the same?

NOTES

1. Daniel Goleman, *Emotional Intelligence: Why It Can Matter More Than IQ* (New York: Bantam Books, 1995), 34.
2. Nathan O. Hatch, *The Democratization of American Christianity* (New Haven, CT: Yale University Press, reprint 1991).

16

Reclaiming Our Time

Jay Williams

Jay Williams is lead pastor, Glide Memorial United Methodist Church, San Francisco.

"And now faith, hope, and love abide, these three; and the greatest of these is love."

—1 Corinthians 13:13 NRSV

SO ENDS PAUL'S FAMOUS "love poem," common fare at civil unions and Christian weddings alike. The familiar beginning to this sonnet speaks of tongues and gongs and cymbals and angels. I prefer to start, however, a little bit earlier at the end of the twelfth chapter. There Paul introduces his poem: "I will show you a still more excellent way." This new beginning reframes the journey, and perhaps takes us to a better destination. Yes, there are *other* alternatives in our "way forward." Still, there is something far greater—*more excellent,* even—and that is the way of love.

Walking Contradictions

As an undergraduate I sat in the pews of Boston's Union United Methodist Church, the denomination's first African-American "Reconciling Congregation." During those days, my mentor, the late Bishop Martin David McLee, was Union's pastor: his prophetic voice that called for cessation of church trials in the New York Annual Conference was cultivated at Union. A decade later, as a doctoral student, I stood in Union's pulpit. It was an incredible honor to pastor the people who nurtured my faith as a college student.[1]

I continue to give thanks for both the many joys and many challenges in ministry at Union—some anticipated, others completely unexpected. I knew that my first funeral would be difficult and my first baptism pure bliss. But I never imagined the heartache that I would experience, as a parish pastor, as the denomination struggled over human sexuality.

What do you *really* say to a woman in her twilight years who does not fully love herself because of her sexuality? How do you help wipe away the tears of a young man who cries himself to sleep every night, because he is in love with another man? When does a married same-gender couple start enjoying their holy matrimony, free from the judgment of family and church? These are among the questions that kept me up at night.

Still, so many times I saw relief in the eyes of men and women, old and young, who finally found a black church that truly embraces them and their sexuality—fully, unconditionally. I witnessed sheer surprise when a woman introduces her wife to Union, and members do not bat an eye. I have seen tears flow as LGBTQ folk found the spiritual home for which they searched for years. But I also felt the utter disappointment—and the confusion—of gay couples asked to be married in Union's sanctuary.

I always imagined that being a pastor would mean extending God's blessing to those who yearn for authentic relationship. "The Lord bless you and keep you" (Numbers 6:24). But The United Methodist Church tells me to do otherwise.[2] It is a hard thing not to bless the same people I pray with, study the Bible with, break bread with, and fellowship with. Actually, it broke my heart. Because sexuality is not something to be debated. This "issue" has faces and stories, disappointments and agonies, hopes and prayers. As a pastor, I have learned that ministry is more about people than policies.

Although the people of Union are not all of one mind, there is something that all have come to know: Union's DNA is made up of the double helix of biblical faith and social justice. Since the congregation's beginnings in 1796, its members have been abolitionists, desegregationists, women's rights advocates, civil rights activists, anti-apartheid protestors, and economic equality seekers. All these issues are tied up in Christ's invitation for us to be reconciled and to be set free. As Union struggled to find its way forward as a congregation, they covenanted to stay at the table as Union seeks a table for all. The people gather as broken vessels around a broken loaf—as one. Because too many people have been hurt, Union decided no longer to fight over "the issue." Union now blesses all its people and their unions—fully, unconditionally.

Traveling the road as Union's pastor (while a Ph.D. student) was both challenging and complicated, and occasionally a walking contradiction. The painfully ironic thing is that I was appointed by the general superintendent (bishop) to a "Reconciling Church" and then ordered by the denomination not to pastor all my people fairly. As a black man in the United States, I know that the "separate but equal" thing simply does not work.[3]

The biggest contradiction for me, though, was the denial of my own self. For years, I tried to keep separate the various constituents of my identity—pastor here, queer man over there. I struggled to keep these selves segregated and managed to do so (or so I thought) for three-and-a-half years. But a few days before Pentecost Sunday 2016, the sermon title "Waiting to Exhale" dropped into my spirit.[4] As I outlined a message about Spirit-as-breath-of-God, I realized that *I* was the one not breathing. I was suffocating for lack of honesty, pretending to be other than I am. And I could take it no longer.

After powerful music and dance ministries, I stood before my people to speak my truth with trembling voice. In a dramatic prolegomenon I confessed:

> For as long as I can remember I have known in my heart of hearts that I am different. Even as a child, I've known. But it was not safe to breathe . . . I was forced to hide my being and I have been suffocating inside . . . dying inside because I have failed to take in fresh air; today I choose a more excellent way. I've been waiting to exhale, but today I breathe again. [Take a deep breath.] Today, today I speak my truth . . . today I come out . . . today I am "called out"[5] . . . And today, I am proud to say that I am gay.

And without skipping a beat (almost as if she had my manuscript), Miss Olivia blurted out in black church call-and-response fashion: "We already knew!"

With laughter and tears, my congregation came and embraced me in light of my not–breaking news. I wept bitterly tears of joy and release. We sang, as my flock assured their shepherd that everything would be just fine. Then, I presided over the Lord's Supper—my first Communion—weeping through its entirety.

Good Enough

Two years prior, on Pentecost Sunday 2014 (and the day after my ordination), I had decided not to be a "Jim Crow" pastor. Contradicting official United Methodist Church law, I committed to pastor all my people equally and to officiate at same-sex weddings. I resolved to live out my ordination vow "to seek peace, justice, and freedom for all people."[6] A longtime congregant shared with me: "Pastor, I know that extending marriage equality is the right thing to do. I was raised a certain way, and it is taking me longer to get where I need to be. But if someone is 'good enough' to serve here and tithe here, then that person should be married here too." It took me a while longer, however, to learn how not to discriminate against myself.

Today, I am blessed to stand in the pulpit of Glide Memorial United Methodist Church in San Francisco. Glide is a wonderful, magical place: every Sunday during Celebration, billionaires worship alongside folk who have bottomed out. At the community's core is a fierce commitment to radical inclusion and unconditional love toward all people—and "all means all." Long before the so-called "incompatibility clause" entered the *Discipline* in 1972, in the 1960s Rev. Cecil Williams was officiating at gay weddings and embracing everyone placed on the margins of church and society. For decades this faith community has modeled something extraordinary. Yet and still, this exceptional witness is the most fundamental thing there is: Nothing "will be able to separate us from the love of God that comes to us in Christ Jesus, our Savior" (Romans 8:39).[7] Folk who have been outcast and excluded have learned to love themselves fully, unconditionally—unlearning the hate they internalized and carried in their bodies. They have claimed their divine inheritance to be loved as those created in the very image of a loving God.

Reclaiming My Time

During the 2016 U.S. presidential campaign, the gentle lady from California, 78-year-old U.S. Representative Maxine Moore Waters emerged as a superstar for millennials. In the age of "alternative facts" and lies, millennials have fallen in love with her because she is a brutally honest truth-teller. "Auntie Maxine," as she's been dubbed, has defied the so-called generational divide and has bridged the gap between young and old. She has borne witness to the truth of the psalm: "I once was young, and now I'm old; / but I've never seen the just forsaken" (Psalm 37:25a).

There is perhaps no greater illustration of Waters's dramatic display of agency than her July 2017 confrontation with Steven Mnuchin (U.S. Treasury Secretary). During a congressional hearing regarding Trump's financial ties to Russia, Waters brilliantly exerted control over what's hers—*her time*. When Mnuchin tried to interrupt her and steer the conversation in his favor, over and over again, she interrupted: *"Reclaiming my time… reclaiming my time… reclaiming my time."* (If you haven't seen the exchange, you can find it on YouTube.)

Similarly, Auntie Maxine urges those who have been historically marginalized and silenced to find their voice. Representative Waters declares that she will not be controlled, and that she, and only she, will control her time. And, likewise, she challenges us all to claim our agency; to claim it with urgency; and to claim it in perpetuity.[8] Reclaiming time each day is a daily revolt: it is a protest, a demonstration, an objection to oppression. By reclaiming time we make a conscious decision not to be held captive to systems of power that stand in the way of our flourishing.

Like the biblical Queen Esther (Hadassah), Representative Waters speaks out—speaking against, even—and refuses to be complacent and complicit with injustice. "If you insist on remaining silent at this time, vindication and liberation will come to our people through another source" (Esther

4:14). With Auntie Maxine, we must be the Queen Esthers who use our voice, take hold of our power, and reclaim our time in history.

The Scriptures speak to the importance of resistance against the oppressive powers that be, which seek to perpetuate the status quo. The great prophet from Palestine, Jesus, reclaimed time in a way that helps us reconceive how we spend our time. In the twelfth chapter of the Gospel according to Matthew, we find an account of Jesus confronting the Pharisees. Jesus and his followers, while walking through fields of grain on the sabbath, the day of rest, plucked the grain because they were hungry.

The religious lawyers saw this and criticized Jesus for not following the letter of the law. The Pharisees were concerned with rules and regulations; Jesus was concerned with feeding folk who were hungry. There was food all around, but the lawyers manipulated the meaning of sabbath and said the hungry were not supposed to eat! Jesus calls out this nonsense. He declares: "Something greater than the Temple is here. . . . I desire compassion and empathy, not sacrifices" (Matthew 12:6-7).

The story continues on to explain that Jesus and his disciples then enter the Jewish synagogue and again the Pharisees, the religious lawyers, try to hold Jesus captive to form and fashion—to formulaic, narrow thinking. There is a man in the synagogue with a withered hand and the Pharisees try to trick Jesus and ask, "Is it lawful to heal on the Sabbath?" And Jesus responds, "Which one of you if your sheep were to fall in a ditch on the Sabbath, would not grab it and lift it out? Certainly a person is more valuable than a sheep! So then, yes, it is lawful to do good on the Sabbath" (Matthew 12:10-12).

Jesus rejects any form of gradualism that would cause us to wait for tomorrow for the justice that is due us today.[9] He rejects the control of time that would stand against life. The prophetic Messiah declares that *now* is the time. In a way, Jesus anticipates the declaration of Black Methodists for Church Renewal: "Our time under God is now."

Jesus explains that the Pharisees got the meaning of sabbath twisted: they were manipulating sabbath as an "alternative fact," distorting its meaning. So

Jesus corrects them—he contradicts them, which literally means to "speak against." Sabbath, Jesus teaches, was intended to liberate us, never to hold us captive. Biblical scholar Walter Brueggemann underscores the Exodus point that "Sabbath is resistance." By taking sabbath, we free ourselves from the mentality that we must work all the time in order to prove our worth in the world. According to Brueggemann, sabbath is liberation from the logic that we are defined by labor. Instead, the prophet Jesus declares that we are children of God just as we are. We are loved. We are of inherent, sacred worth and value. And we must not allow anyone to tell us any differently. Sabbath is resistance: we reclaim the time to love ourselves enough to rest.[10]

Jesus embodies holy contradiction! We, too, during these days and for such a time as this, must have the blessed courage to contradict that which stands against the liberating love of God. Father of black liberation theology James Cone is correct: "Now as theologians of the church of Christ if we have difficulty telling the truth, then we ought to choose another profession."[11]

Scriptural Holiness and Unholy Contradictions[12]

The truth is that Scripture has been used for good *and* manipulated to do great harm. And the church has used Scripture to justify a long history of injustice: from slavery and sexism to segregation and heterosexism. During the Civil Rights Movement, two Methodist bishops signed a statement encouraging gradualism and patience in ending segregation. They told folk who were fighting for their lives just to wait a little while longer. Indeed, it is to these two Methodist bishops and six other clergymen that Rev. Dr. Martin Luther King, Jr., addresses his prophetic "Letter from a Birmingham Jail."[13]

It seems that we have also forgotten the first General Rule of the Methodist movement: *Do no harm*. The church continues to do harm each time it says again that some are in and some are out; that some are insiders and some are outsiders; that some are chosen and others rejected. The church does harm each time it favors law over grace. The church does harm and the church forgets the most basic affirmation of the Christian faith: grace trumps the law each and every time. Yes, love liberates us from laws that oppress. In the view of God, there is no such law that prohibits some while accepting others. Because God's law is grace, God's law is *not* church law; God's law is love. The church has no authority that does not come from God. And God is love (1 John 4:8). Full stop. No exceptions. No qualifications. No prerequisites. No fine print.

John Wesley, the founder of Methodism, had no ecclesiastical authority to do what he did to start the Methodist movement. Consequently, his authorization of general superintendents (bishops) was invalid. In my analysis, then, the so-called invalid consecration of Bishop Karen Oliveto stands in pretty good company and emerges from a solid history of resistance.

We should learn from our history and the Christmas Conference of 1784.[14] We should remember that the ordination of Francis Asbury by Thomas Coke, Richard Whatcoat, Thomas Vasey, and Philip Otterbein, and the consecration of Coke and Asbury as bishops, stood outside of ordinary apostolic succession. In other words, it broke with the tradition. Wesley, as an Anglican priest, had no ecclesiastical authority to ordain Coke or to direct other priests to consecrate a bishop. This process simply was *not* how it was done for hundreds of years in apostolic succession. So the consecration of the first two Methodist bishops was "invalid." The United Methodist Church, I believe, must remember its history—and learn from it.

Some are afraid that The United Methodist Church might split. And while this would be tragic, I am not afraid, because in 1844 the Methodist Episcopal Church split over slavery. Slave-owning Christians—an oxymoron if I ever heard one—in the South broke away from antislavery Christians in the North. And two Methodist Churches were formed: The Methodist Episcopal Church and the Methodist Episcopal Church, South. Perhaps institutional brokenness is necessary in order for ethical wholeness to come. Sometimes things must die, as we know them, in order for new life to come. Is this not the message of Easter? And is this not also the message of Pentecost: that the loss of Christ in the Ascension is not a loss at all, but a gain as the Spirit of Christ is poured out on all people for all times?

In 1939, when the abolitionist Methodist Church of the North rejoined with the slave-holding Methodist Church of the South, Negroes were segregated into a Central Jurisdiction. When The Methodist Church finally decided that slavery was evil, many white Methodists still didn't want to pray alongside Negroes. In essence, just like water fountains and bathrooms and sections on public buses, there was a Methodist Church for "whites only" and a Methodist Church for "blacks only."

And then in 1972, The United Methodist Church's prohibition against homosexuality began in the context of the free love and sexual liberation movements of the 1960s and 1970s. For decades since, our denomination has sought not liberation but captivity for citizens it has deemed second-class.

Here's the point: The United Methodist Church's current discrimination against LGBTQ folk comes out of a long tradition of Methodist discrimination—injustice—a history that we have tried to forget. The history of The United Methodist Church is a living example of a church that has been on the wrong side of history.

We must remember. When we remember history and read the Bible in context, we learn two fundamental facts: While God is always right, the church can be wrong. And the Bible is not God's Word, Jesus is.

Now don't get me wrong, the Bible is beautiful. I read the Bible every day, and pray that it is written upon the tablets of my heart (Proverbs 7:3). But the Bible is complicated. In fact, *the* Bible is not a single book, but rather a collection of books. And as such, it says some crazy stuff:

- The Bible says that eating shellfish is an abomination. So during lobster season, remember that (Leviticus 11:10-12).
- The Bible says that women on their menstrual cycles were not to be touched, because they were "unclean" (Leviticus 15:19-33).
- The Bible says women should be silent in church (1 Corinthians 14:34).

- The Bible says in our beloved Exodus story that genocide against native people is permissible—God-sanctioned, even (Deuteronomy 1:8; Numbers 33:53).
- The Bible says slaves must obey masters (1 Peter 2:18-22; Colossians 3:22; Ephesians 6:5-9).

So the Bible must always be read in context. And whenever it is dis-connected from the circumstances that gave it rise, we risk dis-remembering—forgetting—the power of its words.[15]

Let me make it plain: Jesus uttered not a word of condemnation toward queer people. Despite the scriptural support for heteronormativity, we must remember that Jesus did not read the Bible—because the Bible had not been written! And more important, Jesus is the Word of God.[16] The Bible gives us clues to Jesus, who is God-consciousness; but the totality of Jesus, who is the Word of God, always transcends what we find written in human words. Why? Because God is still speaking and showing up in the world wherever Jesus is. And the Bible itself testifies to this very fact: "For my thoughts are not your thoughts, / nor are your ways, my ways,' says YHWH" (Isaiah 55:8).

So, what if we start this homosexuality debate a little bit earlier—a little earlier in time? We might realize that we have been down this road before in the church with regard to slavery. We overcame this injustice, figuring out a way to read holy writ in such a way that does not hold us captive to narrow thinking. Like Jesus, in search of that more excellent way, we must sometimes read against and speak against the text. Indeed that's why we speak of *con*text. And we can do so again if we want to: it is a matter of will. Yes, we can "become again what we never were,"[17] or never were allowed to be.

Jesus Is Love

The great American poet Langston Hughes, a queer black man, once penned in his poem "Let America Be America Again": "Let it be the dream it used to be. . . . Let it be that strong land of love."[18] Like Paul's poem, Hughes calls us to that greatest of virtues: love. We might put behind us past days and childish ways and step boldly into the fullness of who we are created to be: children of love. Unfortunately, like Langston's America, The United Methodist Church has never fully been what it promised to be. It has called me, and other beloved of God, "incompatible," a scar that for too long we have carried in our bodies. Deemed an unholy ghost, I have been haunted by this legacy.

Still, I cling to the promise made when I was welcomed into the body of Christ: "to renounce the spiritual forces of wickedness . . . [to] accept the freedom and power God gives [me] to resist evil, injustice, and oppression in whatever forms they present themselves."[19] How prophetic our baptismal vow: our Methodist history shows us that injustice finds itself in the church, too. And when injustice is found, we are called to contradict—to speak against—it. For such a time as this, we who have been silenced can no longer keep silence.

One of Union's favorite songs is the 1980 Commodores hit "Jesus Is Love." Without fail, every time it is sung, the congregation is up swaying with uplifted hands. Before long, worshipers have joined in the refrain: "yeah, yeah, Jesus loves you." In many ways, this song reflects Union's radical character. And it is the foundation of how I live as a pastor and scholar. Jesus, the liberating Spirit of God, is love.

My prayer is that there be more Unions and Glides out there. Like the song's opening lyrics: "Father [Mother], help your children." All of us. I hope the church truly learns to live in liberation, or it will face obsolescence. The brilliant work of art and 2017 Academy Award–winning film, *Moonlight*, serves as writing on the wall (Daniel 5:1-30).[20] Although baptism and revelation figure prominently in this triadic coming of age story of a black gay male, there is no mention of the church. If we do not get it right, this erasure will move from silver screen to real life.

NOTES

1. An earlier version of this section appears in "Sharing in Faith: Jesus is Love": http://www.umc.org/what-we-believe/sharing-in-faith-jesus-is-love

(2014) and the preface to my dissertation *Unholy Ghosts in the Age of Spirit: Identity, Intersectionality, and the Theological Horizons of Black Progress* (Harvard University, May 2017, unpublished).

2. *The Book of Discipline of The United Methodist Church, 2016,* states: "The practice of homosexuality is incompatible with Christian teaching. Therefore self-avowed practicing homosexuals are not to be certified as candidates, ordained as ministers, or appointed to serve in The United Methodist Church" (¶304.3). Also: "Ceremonies that celebrate homosexual unions shall not be conducted by our ministers and shall not be conducted in our churches" (¶341.6). *The Book of Discipline of The United Methodist Church* (Nashville: The United Methodist Publishing House, 2016), 226, 278.
3. The decision of the National Association for the Advancement of Colored People to pursue a legal end to segregation, which led to *Brown v. Board of Education of Topeka* that overturned *Plessy v. Ferguson* as unconstitutional, was taken at the annual meeting held at Union Methodist Episcopal Church (now Union United Methodist Church), June 20-25, 1950. http://americanhistory.si.edu/brown/history/3-organized/turning-point.html. Accessed August 15, 2017.
4. See Terry McMillan's *Waiting to Exhale* (New York: Viking, 1992) and the film of the same title (Los Angeles: Twentieth Century Fox Home Entertainment, 1999).
5. "Called Out" is a movement of LGBTQI Clergy in The United Methodist Church to declare publicly their sexual orientation, in opposition to the denomination's anti-gay posture and the potential punitive repercussions, which include defrocking. http://www.rmnetwork.org/newrmn/calledout/. Accessed March 30, 2017.
6. *Services for the Ordering of Ministry in The United Methodist Church,* 2013-2016 as Revised by Action of the 2012 General Conference, copyright © 1998, 2000, 2002, 2006, 2008, 2012, The United Methodist Publishing House.
7. Remaining scriptural verses come from *The Inclusive Bible: The First Egalitarian Translation* (Lanham: Rowman & Littlefield Publishers, 2007).
8. See also Michael Hanchard, "Afro-Modernity: Temporality, Politics, and the African Diaspora," *Public Culture* 11 (1999), 245–268.
9. See also Martin Luther King, Jr., *Why We Can't Wait* (New York: Harper & Row, 1964).
10. Walter Brueggemann, *Sabbath as Resistance: Saying No to the Culture of Now* (Westminster John Knox Press, 2014).

11. James H. Cone, "The Vocation of a Theologian." Excerpts from an address at the fall convocation at Candler School of Theology published in *Union News,* Union Theological Seminary, Winter 1991.
12. An earlier version of a portion of this section was preached at the Service of Remembrance of the 218th Session of the New York Annual Conference of The United Methodist Church (June 8, 2017): http://www.nyac.com/files/tables/content/8448541/files/Dangerous-Disremembering-Rev-Jay-Williams-NYAC-2017-Memorial-Service-final-manuscript.pdf. Accessed December 1, 2017.
13. See "An Appeal for Law and Order and Common Sense" (January 16, 1963) and "Unwise and Untimely: A Letter from Eight Alabama Clergymen" (April 12, 1963), both signed by Bishop Paul Hardin of the Alabama-West Florida Conference and Bishop Nolan B. Harmon of the North Alabama Conference of The Methodist Church. http://www.thekingcenter.org/archive/document/unwise-and-untimely. Accessed September 1, 2017.
14. "A Brief History of The United Methodist Church," *The Book of Discipline of The United Methodist Church* (Nashville: The United Methodist Publishing House, 2016), 11–24. Cf. Richard P. Heitzenrater, *Wesley and the People Called Methodists* (Nashville: Abingdon Press, 1995), 261–308.
15. Toni Morrison, *Beloved,* 1987 (New York: Plume: 1988), 274.
16. Remember that Our Doctrinal Standards, in particular the "Confession of Faith of the Evangelical United Brethren Church," states plainly in Article IV: "We believe the Holy Bible, Old and New Testaments, reveals the Word of God" (¶104). *The Book of Discipline of The United Methodist Church,* 73.
17. Michel Foucault, *The Hermeneutics of the Subject: Lectures at the Collège de France,* 1981-1982, trans. Graham Burchell (New York: Picador, 2005), 95.
18. Langston Hughes, "Let America Be America Again," *The Collected Works of Langston Hughes, Volume I: The Poems, 1921-1940,* ed. Arnold Rampersad (Columbia: University of Missouri Press, 2001), 131–132.
19. "The Baptismal Covenant I," *The United Methodist Hymnal* (Nashville: The United Methodist Publishing House, 1989), 34; *The United Methodist Book of Worship* (Nashville: The United Methodist Publishing House, 1992), 88.
20. *Moonlight* (released October 21, 2016). Screenplay by Barry Jenkins, Story by Tarell Alvin McCraney. A24, Plan B Entertainment, Pastel Productions.

17

Toward the Healing of United Methodist Divisions

J. Philip Wogaman

J. Philip Wogaman is former senior minister at Foundry United Methodist Church and former professor of Christian Ethics at Wesley Theological Seminary, both in Washington, D.C.

DIVISION IS NOT A NEW THING in the Wesleyan tradition. The United Methodist Church and its predecessor denominations went through deep conflicts and divisions almost from the beginning. Divisions in two of the predecessor denominations (Methodist Episcopal Church, then The Methodist Church) include split-offs to form AME and AME Zion and Methodist Protestant denominations, deep disputes over slavery, division between north and south in the 1840s, splits resulting in Wesleyan Methodist and Nazarene denominations, disputes over women's ordination, racial segregation, and so on and on.

Conflict is not new in our denomination.

Still, the debates over same-gender relationships have been especially acrimonious. Beginning in 1972 the General Conference of the newly formed United Methodist Church singled out homosexual activity for special condemnation. The General Conferences of 1984 and 1996 prohibited the ordination and appointment of "self-avowed, practicing homosexuals" and made it a chargeable offense for UM clergy to officiate at same-gender weddings. All of these moves, though reaffirmed by successive General Conferences, were stoutly resisted by a substantial body of delegates.

The root of the division is not simply structural. It is based on deep-seated theological and ethical differences. I believe the basic issue is presented by the words in the *Book of Discipline* adopted in 1972: "The United Methodist Church does not condone the practice of homosexuality and considers this practice incompatible with Christian teaching" (par. 161G).The Social Principles include commitment to welcome and love everybody and goes on to "implore families and churches not to reject or condemn lesbian and gay members and friends." Still, the condemnation of "the practice of homosexuality" remains. And this has provided the basis for the provisions in church law affecting clergy.

I am struck by the fact that the *Discipline* does not provide reasons for the conclusion that "homosexual practice" is incompatible with Christian teaching. Which teachings? A small number of scriptural passages can be, and often are, cited. Perhaps the most important of these is Romans 1 where Paul lists various evidences of "degrading passions," including same-gender sexual acts. Citing this and the other passages as "proof texts" runs into immediate difficulties, including lack of theological rationale for the conclusions. Moreover, if we cite a specific moral teaching as absolute authority simply because it is in the Bible, we have implicitly committed ourselves to accepting *all* scriptural teachings as binding. Even biblical literalists don't accept the draconian penalties of, say, Leviticus as any longer binding. And those who want to limit such authority to New Testament teachings have to confront such teachings as that women should not speak in church (much less lead worship!): "Let a woman learn in silence with full submission. I permit no woman to teach or to have authority over a man; she is to keep silent" (1 Timothy 2:11-12 NRSV). I suspect that a kind of natural law ethic is really involved among those who cite Christian teaching. Same-gender sexual relations seems on the face of it to be contrary to nature. That may have seemed quite true centuries ago, but it is more than doubtful today.

Such points aside, the phrase "incompatible with Christian teaching" has labeled same-gender sexual relationships as a form of sin. In the church's debates over such relationships, I wish our differences and possible agreements about the nature of sin could be discussed more clearly.

What Is Sin?

Many people (perhaps most?) think of particular "sins"—this or that action, practice, or attitude that is considered to be sinful. Thus, in an earlier era many Methodists thought of dancing, playing cards, going to movies (especially on Sunday), drinking alcoholic beverages, and swearing as sins. Divorce and premarital sex definitely qualified. Insofar as reasons could be given, they often came down to such things as violation of rules. Among ethicists, this is understood to be a prescriptive form of ethics. The hallmark of this approach to ethics is whether or not we obey commandments, laws, rules, and so on that have come to us from authoritative sources. Sin is disobedience to divine authority. We have disobeyed God, who set forth the requirements for our salvation. The Ten Commandments and other rules and laws contained in Scripture are central. Thus, in the case of homosexuality, the teachings in the Bible, though few in number, are decisive.

I find this view embedded in the April 2017 United Methodist Judicial Council ruling about same-gender marriage. The council, following *Discipline* par. 304.3, held that a person is ineligible for ordination if he or she is a "self-avowed practicing homosexual" because a candidate for ministry is "required to maintain the highest standards of holy living in the world." So homosexual practice is identified here as inconsistent with "highest standards of holy living." Holiness is not here defined, but its opposite can be understood as sin. The Judicial Council ruled that being in a same-sex marriage is, in fact, being a self-avowed practicing homosexual. It thus would seem that being in such a relationship is tantamount to living in sin. Neither the *Discipline* nor the Judicial Council overlooked the reality of human imperfection, for par. 304.3 acknowledges the frailty of all humanity. But that very acknowledgment seems to mean that "homosexual practice" is especially important, going beyond the limits of common human frailty. This is not ordinary sin; it is especially grave.

We return to the question, Why? I believe further discussions within the church, as we seek to surmount the present impasse, should focus exactly at that point. Why is this sinful? And if it is sinful, why should it be singled out for special emphasis?

As a contribution to that discussion, I wish to offer a somewhat different view of what *sin* means. Among theologians, at least from St. Augustine on, sin is often treated as a condition rather than a catalog of forbidden acts. Specific acts, labeled as "sins," are a result of the deeper condition of sinfulness. The condition, broadly understood, is alienation from God, sometimes expressed as rebellion against God. So separation from God is the heart of the matter. The question then is whether there is something about "homosexual practice" that *necessarily* constitutes alienation from God or separation from God. In Christian tradition some portrayals of God stress God's anger, God's wrath in the face of human sin, and that God will punish us for our condition of sin with its resultant acts of sin.

There is theological tension between a view of God that stresses commandments and judgment, with rewards and punishments, and faith in God's grace as revealed in Jesus Christ. The latter can be understood as God's unconditional love for us despite our sin, despite our imperfections. But the tension between the two is suggested by Bonhoeffer's invective against "cheap grace." He writes that this is "Grace without price; grace without cost! . . . I can go and sin as much as I like, and rely on this grace to forgive me, for after all the world is justified in principle by grace."[1] Grace does not come without cost. But that cannot mean that we have to *earn* grace, to *earn* the love of God. St. Paul was pretty clear about that in his view that grace is prior to law. Can we really depend upon God's unconditional love?

I believe the tension can be resolved in this way: God's love is at the heart of our faith. None of us really deserves it; there is no way we can earn it. It is simply given. *But* our ability to *receive* God's grace is limited by our sin. The consequence of human freedom is that we can create barriers to the receiving of the love of God. A human analogy: Parents may love their children unconditionally. Nothing could make them not love their children. But, perhaps especially in some of the teenage years, a child may not experience that love. It is not necessarily the parents' fault, it is the growing child's attitude. That's not so unusual, but typically a child grows through that and comes to see that the parents' love really was always there. Imperfect as this analogy is, I believe it is true of our faith in God. God's love is always there, but in our sinfulness we can create barriers.

What are the consequences of this in our understanding of sexual sin? This now becomes a factual question. Is there anything about sexual attitudes and practices that factually stands in the way of our experiencing the freely given love of God?

It surely can be so. The admonitions against sexual abuse in the Social Principles point to things "that damage the humanity God has given us as birthright" (*Book of Discipline 2016*, par. 161.I). That includes exploitative behaviors and promiscuity. Exploitation treats other persons as things, not fully human, and ironically diminishes confidence in our own humanity (if the other person is only a thing does that mean that I, as a person, am also only a thing?). Promiscuity is a form of exploitation, but it also has the effect of centering our lives around sex and not around God. That is, lurking beneath promiscuity there is idolatry. Such things do stand in the way of our fully experiencing the love of God. Again, it is not that the love of God isn't there; it is that we've erected barriers.

Now the key question: Is there anything about "homosexual practice" that intrinsically and necessarily constitutes such a barrier? That question is at the very heart of our current debates, whether we recognize it or not. And that is a question that turns, finally, on matters of fact. I recognize as fact that homosexual behavior *can* be an expression of sin, as I have defined it here. It is also a fact, of course, that different forms of heterosexual behavior can also be an expression of sin. The key question may well be whether particular sexual expressions are in the service of real love.

But is it *necessarily* so about homosexual "practice"? The *Discipline*'s sweeping words about this as incompatible with Christian teaching imply that that is so—that *all* homosexual practices are *necessarily,* and *always* sinful.

There is a lot of evidence that that is not so! In my own pastoral experience I have known LGBT people who manifest the gifts and graces of Christian life at least to the degree that I find this in heterosexual persons. I state that as observed fact. That is especially the case with the marriages of such people who, after all, make the same commitments of mutual caring "until death do us part." The U.S. Supreme Court's decision legalizing same-gender marriage expressed this eloquently in Justice Kennedy's words:

> No union is more profound than marriage, for it embodies the highest ideals of love, fidelity, devotion, sacrifice, and family. In forming a marital union, two people become something greater than once they were. . . . It would misunderstand these [homosexual] men and women to say they disrespect the idea of marriage. Their plea is that they do respect it, respect it so deeply that they seek to find its fulfillments for themselves. Their hope is not to be condemned to live in loneliness, excluded from one of civilization's oldest institutions.[2]

Those are words of the secular Supreme Court, not the church. But has the Court understood the moral reality here better than The United Methodist Church? I believe so.

Can There Be a Way Forward?

But there are those, I know, who do not believe so. The divisions are so deep, often so acrimonious. Above all, the Wesleyan way is the way of love. Can there be a way for us to express love across the dividing walls? I do not think we will quickly resolve the underlying theological/ethical disputes. The "state of the question" remains open, unresolved, and will probably continue to be for some time ahead. How can we proceed with mutual respect, and even with love, during a time when we all seek greater discernment?

Can't we now accept the good faith of those who disagree with us, and can't we let that be the guiding principle as we reform church law? There may come a time—I believe there will—when there is a broad enough, deep enough consensus on these issues for us to proceed with generally accepted church law. But we are not there yet. On these matters of grave theological concern, majority votes by a General Conference cannot express the soul of the church. Current majorities have determined outcomes that have, for years, been rejected by a very substantial, theologically committed, minority. The effect is to create growing disrespect for church law itself. Thomas Aquinas observed that a ruler should not force conclusions that are not accepted by large numbers of people, for the effect is to diminish rule itself. I can imagine that without change there will be increasing waves of ecclesial disobedience. In the long run, unenforceable church law diminishes respect for all church law.

I would change the "incompatible" language of the Social Principles, either by eliminating it altogether or by substituting language that acknowledges our differences. One example of that might be the words of the 1988 General Conference resolution establishing the Committee to Study Homosexuality—the one time, to my knowledge, that a General Conference has stated what is obviously true: "Whereas, the interpretation of homosexuality has proved to be particularly troubling to conscientious Christians of differing opinion; and Whereas, important biblical, theological, and scientific questions related to homosexuality remain in dispute among persons of good will . . . "[3]

On the matter of UM clergy officiating at same-gender weddings, I would eliminate that prohibition, observing that no UM minister is required to officiate at any particular wedding and that such a pastoral service should not be required of any clergy. I hope the church as a whole might recognize the moral dignity of many same-gender marriages, as the U.S. Supreme Court has clearly done.

In respect to the ordination of "self-avowed, practicing homosexuals," I would eliminate that language. We have, at least until the recent Judicial Council decisions, functioned reasonably well with a kind of "don't ask, don't tell" policy. I can see why numbers of gay and lesbian clergy are increasingly uncomfortable with that, for it means that they cannot be fully honest with others. It becomes an issue of integrity. Again, I've known ministers who were "in the closet" and functioning quite acceptably, even excellently as respected, morally self-disciplined pastors. But here we remember that annual conference Boards of Ordained Ministry can examine candidates with care and propose for ordination and conference membership only those whom they find acceptable. I deplore the current sweeping prohibition (in place only since 1984), but I think it is quite reasonable for a Board of Ordained Ministry to be sure that candidates are morally self-disciplined in their expression of sexuality. Some conferences may continue to treat that in the current sweeping terms, but that should not be mandated for all conferences by church law.

Some voices, both on the "right" and on the "left," seek a denominational split. If that were to entail a total separation, in the manner of the north/south division in the 1840s, it is to be avoided if at all possible. Conceivably greater regional or national forms of relative autonomy could be fashioned. But I'd prefer the kinds of mutual respect I've suggested here, for there remain broad areas of agreement, mutual respect, and institutional effectiveness that need to be preserved.

The one price we ought not be willing to pay is for good people to be stigmatized, through the teaching and law of the church as a whole, as uniquely sinful.

NOTES

1. Dietrich Bonhoeffer, *The Cost of Discipleship* (New York: Macmillan 1937; Touchstone 1995), 48, 50.
2. Justice Anthony Kennedy, www.washingtonpost.com/news/wonk/wp/2015/06/26/the-one-supreme-court-paragraph-on-love-that-gay-marriage-supporters-will-never-forget/?utm_term=.e09d5aa979cb. Accessed November 21, 2017.
3. "History Of The Church's Struggle With The Issue Of Homosexuality"; http://www.archives.soulforce.org/1998/01/01/history-of-policies-on-homosexuality-in-the-united-methodist-church/. Accessed November 21, 2017.